THE
OPEN
FIRE
COOKBOOK

13-Digit ISBN: 978-1-64643-414-5
10-Digit ISBN: 1-64643-414-5

This book may be ordered by mail from the publisher. Please include $5.99 for postage and handling.

Please support your local bookseller first!

Books published by Cider Mill Press Book Publishers are available at special discounts for bulk purchases in the United States by corporations, institutions, and other organizations. For more information, please contact the publisher.

Cider Mill Press Book Publishers
"Where good books are ready for press"

501 Nelson Place
Nashville, Tennessee 37214

cidermillpress.com

Typography: Museo Sans, Flintstock

Pages 45, 52, 71, 76, 84, 88, 95, 96, 108–109, 114, 117, 125, 126, 146, 150–151, 153, 156–157, 152–153, 170–171, 220–221, and 232 courtesy of Cider Mill Press.
All other photos used under official license from Shutterstock.com.

Printed in Malaysia

23 24 25 26 27 OFF 5 4 3 2 1
First Edition

THE
OPEN
FIRE
COOKBOOK

OVER 100 RUSTIC RECIPES
FOR OUTDOOR COOKING

CIDER MILL PRESS

BOOK PUBLISHERS

CONTENTS

Introduction ——————————— 6

Building & Tending a Fire ————— 10

Tools ———————————————— 14

Beef & Lamb —————————— 16

Poultry & Pork ————————— 66

Seafood ——————————— 104

Appetizers, Sides & Salads ———— 142

Rubs, Marinades, Sauces & Stocks — 194

Index ——————————————— 251

INTRODUCTION

Compared to preparing a meal on the stove or in the oven, never mind a microwave or crockpot, cooking over fire is hard work.

But it is also a form of luxury. For everything else becomes ancillary. A great meal prepared over fire is not something one can stumble into, improvise in the course of a busy day, or half-pay attention to. It requires forethought, careful consideration, significant time, unflagging attention.

One must gather the wood. One must select ingredients that justify the effort necessary to build the fire. Once it is lit, one must stand by so that it reaches the ideal level of controlled chaos, neither goes out nor gets out of hand. When the food goes on, the real work begins: making sure the power of the fire does not ruin the food before the smoke can enhance it.

These parameters open spaces that are too often closed off. The search for kindling turns into a walk in the woods. The period waiting for wood to become coals is spent in silent contemplation. The warm glow of the fire invites others to approach, fostering connections and conversations typically off-limits.

And, once the cooking commences, one must become wholly alive, training each sense upon the grill. What is happening to the meat? What color is the smoke rising from it? What is the fire doing? What size and shape log does it need? How does the fire sound? Pay attention as you go to reposition that salmon fillet—has the hot spot shifted somewhere else? Cooking over fire is an illuminating blend of science and art—a process of observing and interrogating what is happening before you, and then using the reflexes instilled by experience to fashion the correct response.

Consistency is everything in cooking, and fire is consistency's sworn enemy. It is unreliable, ever-changing. Capable of lashing out and ruining food in one instant, failing to supply enough heat in the very same spot in another.

Whatever end one envisions for an ingredient, fire is set on complicating that aim. The hot and cool spots will shift every 10 minutes or so, forcing one to not just be focused on the food that has been placed on the grill, but also what the temperature is in a certain spot compared to when you were there last. You cannot let the fire get too low, but you also need to make sure it does not get too hot, that the coal bed retains its level, that the grate is at the proper height. Sometimes, you need to remove every ember beneath a piece of meat, relying on time and ambient heat to get the interior where you want it. Then, for the very same piece of meat, a brief spell over blistering heat is required to get the browned crust that instantly signals "delicious."

Such volatility and variation are far from ideal cooking conditions, but they are incredibly energizing. You cannot grow complacent or disenchanted cooking over fire, you cannot rely on formulas or reputation, or make assumptions about what will happen. It might be less stressful to have such safety nets in place, but they are also the enemies of creativity, preventing one from

paying attention to the present moment, and extinguishing the passion necessary to power through the endless repetitions that cooking entails. Cooking over fire is a wonderful combination of ritual and mystery, where one follows the rote to get to a place where they know nothing. Like any worthwhile practice, it is mysterious and dynamic enough to fill each day with realizations, discoveries, and possibilities.

You will not be able to control it, but so long as you let the fire lead, you can dance with it.

To cook well over a fire, equally large measures of feel, expertise, and dedication are required. These can only be built over time, by standing beside hundreds of fires, learning how to gauge the heat in each section with a quick pass of the hand, becoming able to judge an unseasoned log by its weight, understanding what the color of the smoke issuing from a piece of meat is telling you. Such a lengthy apprenticeship is possible to get through only with passion,

but so long as you have that, and keep a few simple precepts in mind, you will manage.

People tend to equate fire with masculinity. Add meat into the equation and this macho conception gets pushed even further to the extreme, causing people to view grilling as a brief endeavor, where meat must be branded with the all-important sear before the potent flames can damage it completely. With this approach, standing by the grill becomes an anxious vigil, where the "leader of a clan" stands by, watching closely, hoping that they manage to intercede at precisely the right moment.

Instead, the power of fire means you want to be gentle, to go slowly, to be patient, to keep some distance between the coals and the ingredients—particularly when cooking meat.

Meat, you'll recall, is a muscle.

Imagine, for a moment, that you are on an airplane. You've been cruising along smoothly for the past hour, eyes closed and headphones in.

Unexpectedly, the plane enters a pocket of turbulence, causing it to dip suddenly and shudder violently. After a few minutes, the plane gets through the rough patch and resumes making its way placidly toward the destination. But this rediscovered calm does not immediately translate to you. Without fail, entertaining the ultimate consequences of such turbulence will leave your body tense and rigid for a time.

That is what happens to meat when it is placed in a spot where either the flames or improperly high heat can get at it. As a tumultuous stretch 30,000 feet above sea level is an extreme environment for you, so is a ripping-hot grill for a piece of meat. It does not mind a bit of heat. But too much will send it into shock, contracting the muscle's fibers and removing all possibility of it attaining the tender, delicious result you envisioned when you brought it home.

To combat the inclination to strong-arm what goes on the grill, remember this: when grilling, you do not want the flames. Allowing them to make contact with what you're cooking will result in a charred exterior too acrid for anyone to enjoy, and an interior that is undercooked, unappetizing, and potentially harmful.

What you want is the smoke. The purpose of building a fire to cook over is not to exploit its tremendous power to make what was raw quickly edible, but to infuse whatever you are cooking with the sweet, earthy, and pleasantly bitter flavor of its spirit, the smoke.

We can hear you pleading: But what about the sear?

The sear: the brown, crusty exterior that is the first thing most think of when it comes to grilling.

We are not saying that the sear is not important.

We are saying that this too needs to be worked up to slowly. For the sear also makes the meat less vulnerable, preventing heat from getting at the interior with the same efficiency, and keeping the delicious smoke out. If it is granted too quickly, you are going to struggle to get the inside of the meat cooked through without that lovely exterior sliding from browned to burnt, from a crispy, delectable bit of contrasting texture to an unappealing casing. Light charring is fine, but if it goes beyond that, recook the steak.

This browning, known in the cooking world as the Maillard reaction, is the result of proteins and sugars reformulating as new compounds when exposed to heat, introducing new aromas and flavors to the proceedings. It is an essential part of enjoying meat, but even this miraculous transformation takes a back seat to what is conferred by the smoke.

As cooking over an open fire is about controlling exposure to heat, you need to be able to gauge that heat. Even if you do not use the setup recommended in the Building & Tending a Fire section (see page 10), the heat issuing from the coals is not going to be uniform. It is going to be tepid in some spots and blistering in others, and identifying where these are, and which areas lie somewhere between, is essential. Generally, you can determine the heat in each section of the grill by placing your hand right above the grate.

- Extremely high heat is present in any spot you cannot leave your hand over for even two seconds.

- High heat will allow for the hand to remain for two seconds before you need to moveit away.

- Medium heat accommodates you for five seconds, and low dwells in a zone where your hand is OK for nine or so. Testing the grill to determine where these temperatures reside, and checking in on them frequently, will let you know where an ingredient should start—high for fish fillets and thinner cuts, low for thick pieces of meat, vegetables, and whole fish—and how to adjust if an ingredient communicates that it isn't in the right spot.

Touching the meat to determine whether it is properly cooked is another indispensable habit to develop. When you are a true pro, you will be able to tell what's going on inside simply by pressing down with your tongs. But before you have this feel, it's good to be hands on. A good, ahem, rule of thumb is to put each of your fingertips (one at a time) against the tip of your thumb, and use the index finger on your other hand to press against the pad below the thumb. The changes in how that pad feels for each finger will let you know what the various levels of doneness are for meat— the pinkie is well-done, the ring finger is medium-well, the middle finger is medium, and the index finger is what a medium-rare piece of meat should feel like.

It is also important to monitor the color of the smoke issuing from the food. So long as you see gray or blue smoke, you are OK. The second you see white smoke, transfer whatever you are grilling to a cooler spot on the grill, as that pale smoke indicates that it is starting to burn. It may already be too late, but if you act quickly, you should be able to salvage the meal.

The grate should be scraped clean with a wire brush before any meat is placed on it, as the carbonized remains from your last session will lend whatever you are cooking an unpleasant bitterness. During longer cooks, it's not a terrible idea to give it an occasional scrub between rounds, as fat

can build up on the metal and encourage flare-ups. Though frequent grilling will season the grate (much like a cast-iron pan) and prevent food from sticking, for leaner cuts, it is perfectly fine to brush it with a bit of olive or canola oil.

Following these tips will not make you a master, but they will put you in position to avoid disaster, and sustain your enthusiasm. Do your best to keep them in mind, and reread this section often until they are ingrained.

Above all else, remember: your job is to care for the fire. Should the fire go out, all that time and energy will be for naught, all your grand plans dashed. Should the fire get out of control, your home, and your life, may be imperiled. You have been charged not only with cooking, but with caretaking. Act accordingly.

BUILDING & TENDING A FIRE

If you're going to build a fire to cook a meal over, calculate that it will take at least an hour to ensure a bed of coals suitable for cooking. If you're only cooking one steak, and helping the wood fire out with a bit of charcoal, it won't take that long. At the other end of the spectrum, if you're throwing a huge barbecue and cooking several different cuts of beef, sausages, chicken, and/or fish, you'll want to block out an entire afternoon. (A weekend, really. Between the shopping, gathering of wood, starting the fire, tending the grill, and cleaning up, you're not going to get to much else.) Aside from these exceptions, to get enough embers that you can cook a meal for a medium-size group, an hour is a good length of time to block out. It may not take that long, but to put yourself in position to remain patient and focused throughout the process, it is recommended.

To cook over open fire, you're going to need some wood, but working a bit of charcoal into the mix isn't a bad idea. An all-wood fire requires the most skill, time, and attention, but it will reward with the most flavor. To do this, you'll need a reliable source of wood. This will be more difficult in some places than others, especially in warmer climes where heating via woodstove is not commonplace. Ask around to determine which vendors are trustworthy in your area. If no one's certain, it's worth asking an employee at a solid barbecue spot or an establishment with a wood-fired oven where they procure their wood.

Once you have wood, you need to carve out a space to store it, a place where it will remain dry and continue to season, aka dry out. It's recommended that you provide any wood you purchase with a shelter, and let it dry out for at least six months. This may seem like overkill, but using improperly seasoned wood, often referred to as green, makes it difficult to get the desired temperature, since the heat from the flames will be focused on transforming the excess water in the unseasoned logs into steam, rather than burning the wood and producing coals.

Not everyone has the resources or space to keep 10 cords on-site before they even consider touching it. If that's the case, do your best to buy wood that has already been seasoned for at least six months—most outfits will offer seasoned and green wood, the latter being less expensive. It is also important to make sure that you use wood that has been seasoned naturally rather than in a kiln. Kiln-dried wood is actually too dry to cook with effectively—it will burn hastily, making it very difficult to gain any control over the coal bed, and forcing you to go through wood at a rate that isn't really economically reasonable.

How can you tell whether the inside of a piece of wood is dry enough to

properly fuel a fire? Well, there are tools that can tell you. But the easiest way is simply by feel, judging the weight of the log when you pick it up. As you continue to work with wood, you'll develop a feel for your logs, noticing that the lighter they are, the better. If you reach for a log and it is heavy relative to others of a similar size that you have handled, it is too wet and should be passed over.

As to the type of wood you're going to use in open fire cooking, that's going to depend on what is most plentiful based on where you live. Oak is a great enhancer, bolstering an ingredient's best attributes instead of overwhelming them. Hickory provides a lovely, powerful smoke and burns for a long time. Oak and hickory are hardwoods, which can be categorized as coming from trees that give up their leaves and produce a fruit or nut. You can use any hardwood you'd like and get acceptable results, though mesquite may be too harsh for many palates. Stick to what grows locally, and mix in other hardwoods, if desired, to add another note to your grilling. Using softwoods, wood from trees

that have needles instead of leaves, is to be avoided. A softwood, such as the plentiful pine and spruce, will coat your food in an unappetizing resin that will ruin even a perfectly cooked porterhouse.

If one is going to cook with wood, there are a few arrangements that will be conducive to starting a fire. The first is to place some kindling and scraps of paper in a pile and then make a teepee out of twigs around it, leaning them against one another. Surround the teepee with another teepee made of thicker twigs or thin logs. Slide some newspaper through the openings of the teepee, set it alight, and add larger logs as the fire develops.

The second type of fire structure is a simple box, with two thicker logs positioned on the ground parallel to each other, and two similarly sized placed on top, perpendicular to those on the ground.

Cover the empty space on top with two logs, and slide kindling and paper into the empty space at the bottom. Light the paper and add logs as needed until you have the right amount of coals.

Once the fire is going, you're far from done. It takes time to develop a substantial coal bed with wood, as wood coals burn faster than those resulting from charcoal. Stand by, pour yourself a glass of wine, and be patient. When the coals go from red-hot to covered with white ash, they're ready to be transferred to the grill.

Once you have this coal bed, the best way to control the heat is going to be raising and lowering the grate. You can also produce this effect by banking the coals higher on one side, and gradually reducing the depth of the bed until you have an area with no coals at all. This setup, with the deeper parts of the bed serving as "direct heat," and those sections with few or no coals serving as "indirect heat," will give you zones with hot, medium, and low temperatures. Though this arrangement is most valuable when cooking several different cuts, it will still pay dividends when you are cooking just one steak, allowing you to shift a piece of meat that has browned too fast to a section where the heat is lower, preventing the outside from burning before the inside is cooked.

This approach also allows you to start cooking over low heat, before finishing it over high, which is not always called for, but is a solid approach to default to.

You want to have wood burning in another spot and add fresh coals to your grill, rather than placing fresh logs on the coal bed. Fresh logs on your cook fire will create a lot of flames and a lot of smoke, making it hard to obtain anything like steady temperatures, and potentially shifting the wood from something that improves your food to something that overwhelms it.

In no way is it essential to use this wood-only approach in your own open fire cooking. One could easily start the fire with charcoal and place some wood on top of the coals once they are going— thin branches are particularly good when utilizing a charcoal-forward approach. If one is going to go this route, it is important to remember that the fire will burn hotter than it would with just wood, as all the water has been burned off during the process of turning wood into charcoal. Charcoal will also smoke less than wood, so it won't enhance flavor to the same degree. You'll also want to exclusively use lump charcoal, which is the only option for someone who is serious about cooking over fire. Charcoal briquettes do contain wood, but also additives such as limestone and borax that will interfere with the straightforward, smoky flavor you are after. This suggested avoidance of briquettes goes double for those abominations that are infused with lighter fluid. They severely alter the flavor of the food, freighting each bite with anxiety about the long-term impact it will have on one's health. As you may have anticipated, lighter fluid, and other petroleum-based accelerants, are also a no-go when starting a fire to cook over.

TOOLS

Though there are plenty of options to spend your hard-earned money on, remember that so long as you have fire, the hard work has been done—after that, there are plenty of ways to rig up a workable cooking surface. Maybe you want to dig a pit, surround it with two stacks of bricks, and set a grate on top of them. Maybe want to build an old-school brick barbecue in your backyard. Maybe you want to run down to the nearest hardware store, grab one of the numerous Webers on hand, and get to work. Maybe you have an old steel drum in your garage that can hold the flaming logs, and you only need a grate to put over it. These are all solid options, but for the person who is truly committed to the art of cooking over fire, we strongly, emphatically, recommend an Argentinian-style grill, which is sometimes referred to as the Santa Maria grill. These grills feature a cable or chain that is attached to the grate. Via a crank, the grate can be raised or lowered depending on what is required. If you don't have the resources, space, or interest to head in that direction, the round, classic Weber will work fine, though its thin walls mean you'll burn through a lot more wood and/or charcoal anytime you're putting in a lengthy session.

A sturdy, rectangular grill, like the increasingly popular offering from PK Grill, is a much better option, since the shape makes it much easier to set up your coal bed in a way that provides control over the heat.

Another helpful feature is a grate with sections that can be flipped up, as they make it easier for you to access the coals to reposition or replenish them while cooking. Again, this is not essential, but it does make things easier, and cooking over fire already demands enough of your time and energy.

OTHER TOOLS

CHARCOAL CHIMNEY: Affordable, and priceless. Essential to cooking with charcoal, they can even serve as a makeshift grill on their own—just toss a grate over the top. To use a charcoal chimney, dump the charcoal into the chimney, then stuff a few pieces of paper into the chamber below. Set the chimney down and light the paper. In no time, you'll have red-hot coals.

ROTISSERIE: Not essential, but wonderful for producing a memorable and juicy roast, since the rotisserie allows the ingredient to baste itself. Some grills come with a rotisserie, but a solid one can be purchased for under $100. When using a rotisserie, you want the coal bed to be very hot, and the skewer to be as close to the bed as possible. Place whatever you are cooking in the center of the skewer, and let it go.

GRILL BRUSH: No one, having waited for the coals to attain the proper temperature, wants to clean before cooking. But this is the best time to scrape down the grates, assuming you want your food to taste like what you're cooking, rather than the remains of what you grilled a week ago. A good, simple, strong wire brush makes this crucial bit of tidying a breeze. When the coals are rollicking beneath and the grates are hot, run the brush over them until they are free of burnt matter. For longer sessions, an occasional pass between rounds doesn't hurt.

TONGS: A heavy-duty pair is imperative for repositioning whatever's on the grill, handling the coals beneath, and/or picking up a grate.

HATCHET: A small hatchet with a heavy head will make it much easier to break logs into the smaller pieces that get a fire going. An ax will also work for this task, but a standard hatchet that can flay thin strips of wood from a log will be just fine.

SHOVEL: There's no need to get fancy, but having a dedicated, sturdy shovel for both scooping up coals to replenish the fire and for rearranging the coal bed is a necessity for the open-fire cook. A shovel will also come in handy for those preparations where you need to safely extract a Dutch oven from the coal bed.

LARGE STEEL BUCKET: When the time comes to transfer fresh coals from the auxillary fire to the cook fire, a sturdy steel bucket is essential, making the process easy, and, most importantly, safe.

BEEF & LAMB

Chances are, you purchased this book primarily for the preparations in this chapter. And, considering that the addition of smoke makes the flavor of red meat absolutely perfect, it's an easy stance to understand.

Yield: 2 Servings

Total Time: 1 Hour

NEW YORK STRIP

1 lb. New York strip steak

Salt, to taste

1 tablespoon unsalted butter

I. Season the steak with salt and let it rest at room temperature.

2. Prepare a fire, either setting up an even coal bed if you are able to adjust the height of your grate easily, or banking the coals to set up one zone for direct heat and another for indirect. Set up a grate over the coals.

3. Place your hand over the grate to test the heat in each section. Place the steak over medium heat—a spot you can leave your hand over for 5 seconds before you need to move it away. Cook until the steak is medium-rare (the interior reads 130°F on an instant-read thermometer) and the exterior is nicely seared, 6 to 8 minutes, turning it over just once.

4. Remove the steak from the grill, place the butter on top, and let the steak rest for 2 minutes before serving.

RIB EYE

1 lb. rib eye

2 teaspoons kosher salt

1 tablespoon unsalted butter

1. Season the steak with salt and let it rest at room temperature.

2. Prepare a fire, either setting up an even coal bed if you are able to adjust the height of your grate easily, or banking the coals to set up one zone for direct heat and another for indirect. Set up a grate over the coals.

3. Place your hand over the grate to test the heat in each section. Place the steak over high heat—a spot you can leave your hand over for 2 seconds before you need to move it away. Cook until the steak is medium-rare (the interior reads 130°F on an instant-read thermometer) and the exterior is nicely seared, 6 to 8 minutes, turning it over just once.

4. Remove the steak from the grill, place the butter on top, and let the steak rest for 2 minutes before serving.

Yield: 2 Servings

Total Time: 1 Hour

CHIPOTLE T-BONE

1 tablespoon chipotle chile powder

2 teaspoons kosher salt

1 lb. T-bone steak

2 tablespoons extra-virgin olive oil

I.   Place the chipotle powder and salt in a small bowl and stir to combine. Rub the steak with the olive oil and then coat it with the chipotle mixture. Let the steak rest at room temperature.

2.   Prepare a fire, either setting up an even coal bed if you are able to adjust the height of your grate easily, or banking the coals to set up one zone for direct heat and another for indirect. Set up a grate over the coals.

3.   Place your hand over the grate to test the heat in each section. Place the steak over medium-high heat—a spot you can leave your hand over for 3 or 4 seconds before you need to move it away. Cook until the strip portion of the steak is medium-rare (the interior reads 130°F on an instant-read thermometer) and the exterior is nicely seared, 6 to 8 minutes, turning it over just once.

4.   Remove the steak from the grill and let it rest for 2 minutes before serving.

Yield: 2 to 4 Servings

Total Time: 1 Hour and 45 Minutes

PORTERHOUSE

2 porterhouse steaks, each about 1½ inches thick

2 tablespoons extra-virgin olive oil

Salt and pepper, to taste

I. Rub the steaks with the olive oil, season them with salt, and let them rest at room temperature.

2. Prepare a fire, either setting up an even coal bed if you are able to adjust the height of your grate easily, or banking the coals to set up one zone for direct heat and another for indirect. Set up a grate over the coals.

3. Place your hand over the grate to test the heat in each section. Place the steaks over medium-high heat—a spot you can leave your hand over for 3 to 4 seconds before you need to move it away. Cook until the strip portions of the steaks are medium-rare (the interior reads 130°F on an instant-read thermometer) and the exteriors are nicely seared, 6 to 8 minutes, making sure to turn the steaks over just once.

4. Remove the steaks from the grill, season them with pepper, and let them rest for 2 minutes before serving.

PORTERHOUSE

See page 23

Yield: 2 Servings

Total Time: 1 Hour and 15 Minutes

FLANK STEAK

2 tablespoons extra-virgin olive oil

1 tablespoon chopped fresh rosemary

1 teaspoon fresh thyme

1 to 1½ lb. flank steak

Salt and pepper, to taste

I. Place the olive oil, rosemary, and thyme in a bowl and stir to combine. Rub the steak with the mixture, season it with salt, and let it sit at room temperature.

2. Prepare a fire, either setting up an even coal bed if you are able to adjust the height of your grate easily, or banking the coals to set up one zone for direct heat and another for indirect. Set up a grate over the coals.

3. Place your hand over the grate to test the heat in each section. Place the steak over medium-high heat—a spot you can leave your hand over for 3 or 4 seconds before you need to move it away. Cook until the steak is medium-rare (the interior reads 130°F on an instant-read thermometer), taking care not to overcook it, and the exterior is nicely seared, 6 to 8 minutes, turning it over just once.

4. Remove the steak from the grill, season it with pepper, and let it rest for 2 minutes before slicing it thin against the grain and serving.

Yield: 2 Servings

Total Time: 1 Hour and 30 Minutes

CHILE-RUBBED LONDON BROIL

1 London broil steak, ¾ to 1 inch thick

2 tablespoons extra-virgin olive oil

Chile Rub (see page 199)

1. Rub the steak with the olive oil, apply the rub, and let the steak rest at room temperature.

2. Prepare a fire, either setting up an even coal bed if you are able to adjust the height of your grate easily, or banking the coals to set up one zone for direct heat and another for indirect. Set up a grate over the coals.

3. Place your hand over the grate to test the heat in each section. Place the steak over medium heat—a spot you can leave your hand over for 5 seconds before you need to move it away. Cook until the steak is medium-rare (the interior reads 130°F on an instant-read thermometer) and the exterior is nicely seared, 6 to 8 minutes, turning it over just once.

4. Remove the steak from the grill and let it rest for 2 minutes before slicing and serving.

Yield: 2 Servings

Total Time: 1 Hour

COFFEE-RUBBED SIRLOIN

2 tablespoons finely ground medium roast coffee

2 teaspoons kosher salt

1 lb. top sirloin

1. Place the coffee and salt in a small bowl and stir to combine. Rub the steak with the mixture and let it rest at room temperature.

2. Prepare a fire, either setting up an even coal bed if you are able to adjust the height of your grate easily, or banking the coals to set up one zone for direct heat and another for indirect. Set up a grate over the coals.

3. Place your hand over the grate to test the heat in each section. Place the steak over medium-high heat—a spot you can leave your hand over for 3 or 4 seconds before you need to move it away. Cook until the steak is medium-rare (the interior reads 130°F on an instant-read thermometer) and the exterior is nicely seared, 6 to 8 minutes, turning it over just once.

4. Remove the steak from the grill and let it rest for 2 minutes before serving.

Yield: 2 Servings

Total Time: 1 Hour

FILET MIGNON

1 lb. filet mignon

Salt, to taste

1½ tablespoons unsalted butter

I. Season the steaks with salt and let them sit at room temperature.

2. Prepare a fire, either setting up an even coal bed if you are able to adjust the height of your grate easily, or banking the coals to set up one zone for direct heat and another for indirect. Set up a grate over the coals.

3. Place your hand over the grate to test the heat in each section. Place the steaks over medium heat—a spot you can leave your hand over for 5 seconds before you need to move it away. Cook until the steaks are medium-rare (the interior reads 130°F on an instant-read thermometer) and the exteriors are nicely seared, 12 to 14 minutes, turning them over just once.

4. Remove the steaks from heat, place a pat of butter on top of each one, and let them rest for 2 minutes before serving.

Yield: 2 to 4 Servings

Total Time: 1 Hour and 15 Minutes

STRIP STEAKS WITH PEPPERCORN CREAM SAUCE

2 New York strip steaks, each about 1½ inches thick

2 tablespoons extra-virgin olive oil

Salt, to taste

2 tablespoons freshly ground black pepper

3 tablespoons unsalted butter

1 shallot, minced

½ cup Cognac

½ cup heavy cream

2 tablespoons chopped fresh parsley

1. Rub the steaks with the olive oil and season them with salt. Let them rest at room temperature.

2. Prepare a fire, either setting up an even coal bed if you are able to adjust the height of your grate easily, or banking the coals to set up one zone for direct heat and another for indirect. Set up a grate over the coals.

3. Place your hand over the grate to test the heat in each section. Place the pepper in a small saucepan and place it over medium heat—a spot you can leave your hand over for 5 seconds before you need to move it away—and toast it for 1 minute. Add the butter and shallot and cook, stirring occasionally, until the shallot has softened, about 3 minutes.

4. Remove the pan from heat and add the Cognac. Place the pan back over medium heat and cook until the Cognac has reduced by half. Should the Cognac ignite while it is cooking, shake the pan and wait for the flames to die out.

5. Stir in the cream and cook until the sauce has slightly thickened, 2 to 3 minutes. Stir in the parsley, season the sauce with salt, and remove the pan from heat.

6. Place the steaks over medium-high heat—a spot you can leave your hand over for 3 or 4 seconds before you need to move it away. Cook until the steaks are medium-rare (the interior reads 130°F on an instant-read thermometer) and the exteriors are nicely seared, 6 to 8 minutes. Remove the steaks from the grill and let them rest for 2 minutes.

7. Ladle the sauce over the steaks and enjoy.

RED WINE & HERB TRI-TIP STEAK

2 lbs. tri-tip steak

Red Wine & Herb Marinade (see page 209)

1. Place the steak in a baking dish and pour the marinade over it. Let the steak marinate in the refrigerator overnight.

2. Prepare a fire, either setting up an even coal bed if you are able to adjust the height of your grate easily, or banking the coals to set up one zone for direct heat and another for indirect. Set up a grate over the coals. Remove the steak from the refrigerator and let it rest at room temperature.

3. Place your hand over the grate to test the heat in each section. Place the steak over medium heat—a spot you can leave your hand over for 5 seconds before you need to move it away. Cook until the steak is medium-rare (the interior reads 130°F on an instant-read thermometer) and the exterior is nicely seared, 10 to 12 minutes.

4. Remove the steak from the grill and let it rest for 2 minutes before slicing it thin against the grain and serving.

Yield: 6 Servings

Total Time: 12 hours

BBQ BRISKET

5 lb. center-cut beef brisket

2 tablespoons extra-virgin olive oil

Brisket Rub (see page 205)

Coleslaw (see page 184), for serving

I. Trim any fatty areas on the brisket so that the fat is within approximately ¼ inch of the meat, keeping in mind that it is better to leave too much fat than too little.

2. Rub the brisket with the olive oil and then generously apply the rub, making sure to knead it into the meat. Cover the brisket with plastic wrap and chill it in the refrigerator for 2 hours.

3. Prepare a fire, either setting up an even coal bed if you are able to adjust the height of your grate easily, or banking the coals to set up one zone for direct heat and another for indirect. Set up a grate over the coals.

4. Place your hand over the grate to test the heat in each section. Place the brisket over low heat—a spot you can comfortably leave your hand over for 9 seconds. Cook until the brisket is very tender and the interior temperature is 190°F to 200°F.

5. Remove the brisket from heat and let it rest for 20 to 30 minutes before slicing and serving alongside the Coleslaw.

Yield: 6 to 8 Servings

Total Time: 4 Hours

PRIME RIB

6-rib prime rib roast

3 tablespoons extra-virgin olive oil

4 garlic cloves, minced

1 small shallot, minced

2 tablespoons black pepper

2 tablespoons kosher salt

3 bunches of fresh thyme

3 bunches of fresh rosemary

I. Rub the prime rib with 1 tablespoon of olive oil and let it rest at room temperature for 30 minutes.

2. Place the garlic, shallot, and remaining olive oil in a bowl and stir to combine. Rub the prime rib with the mixture and let it rest at room temperature for another 30 minutes.

3. Prepare a fire, either setting up an even coal bed if you are able to adjust the height of your grate easily, or banking the coals to set up one zone for direct heat and another for indirect. Set up a grate over the coals.

4. Season the prime rib generously with salt and pepper. Take the thyme and rosemary and evenly distribute them between the ribs. Using kitchen twine, secure the bunches of herbs so that they will stay in place when you turn the prime rib while it is cooking.

5. Place your hand over the grate to test the heat in each section. Place the prime rib over medium-low heat—a spot you can leave your hand over for 6 or 7 seconds before you need to move it away. Sear the prime rib all over, about 15 minutes, turning it as necessary.

6. Turn the ribs toward the hottest part of the grill and cook the prime rib until it is charred all over and medium-rare (the interior reads 125°F on an instant-read thermometer), about 2 hours, turning it as necessary.

7. Remove the prime rib from heat and let it rest for 10 minutes before slicing and serving.

BACON CHEESEBURGERS

1 lb. ground beef

1 teaspoon kosher salt

½ teaspoon black pepper

1 egg white

⅓ cup bread crumbs

4 slices of American cheese

8 slices of thick-cut bacon, cooked

Hamburger buns, for serving

I. Prepare a fire, either setting up an even coal bed if you are able to adjust the height of your grate easily, or banking the coals to set up one zone for direct heat and another for indirect. Set up a grate over the coals.

2. Place all of the ingredients, except for the cheese and bacon, in a mixing bowl and work the mixture until well combined. Divide the mixture into four equal parts and form each one into a 1-inch-thick patty.

3. Place your hand over the grate to test the heat in each section. Place the burgers over medium-high heat—a spot you can leave your hand over for 3 or 4 seconds before you need to move it away. Cook for 5 minutes.

4. Flip the burgers over and cook until they are just about cooked through, 4 to 5 minutes.

5. Top each burger with a slice of the cheese and cook until the cheese is melted and the burgers are completely cooked through, 1 to 2 minutes.

6. Remove the burgers from heat, top each one with some of the bacon, and serve on hamburger buns.

Yield: 4 Servings

Total Time: 1 Hour

BBQ BURGERS

1 lb. ground beef

1 teaspoon kosher salt

½ teaspoon white pepper

1 egg white

⅓ cup bread crumbs

4 slices of cheddar cheese

⅓ cup Molasses BBQ Sauce (see page 230)

8 slices of thick-cut bacon, cooked

¼ cup pickled jalapeños

Hamburger buns, for serving

I. Prepare a fire, either setting up an even coal bed if you are able to adjust the height of your grate easily, or banking the coals to set up one zone for direct heat and another for indirect. Set up a grate over the coals.

2. Place the ground beef, salt, pepper, egg white, and bread crumbs in a mixing bowl and work the mixture until well combined. Divide the mixture into four equal parts and form each one into a 1-inch-thick patty.

3. Place your hand over the grate to test the heat in each section. Place the burgers over medium-high heat—a spot you can leave your hand over for 3 or 4 seconds before you need to move it away. Cook for 5 minutes.

4. Flip the burgers over and cook until they are just about cooked through, 4 to 5 minutes.

5. Top each burger with a slice of the cheese and cook until the cheese is melted and the burgers are completely cooked through, 1 to 2 minutes.

6. Remove the burgers from heat, top each one with some of the BBQ sauce, bacon, and jalapeños, and serve on hamburger buns.

BEEF KEBABS

1½ lbs. ground beef

1 onion, grated

1 teaspoon chopped fresh rosemary

3 garlic cloves, minced

1 teaspoon cumin

½ teaspoon dried thyme

Salt and pepper, to taste

I. Prepare a fire, either setting up an even coal bed if you are able to adjust the height of your grate easily, or banking the coals to set up one zone for direct heat and another for indirect. Set up a grate over the coals. If using bamboo skewers, soak them in water.

2. Place all of the ingredients in a mixing bowl and work the mixture with your hands until well combined. Form the meat into an oblong shape around the skewers and chill them in the refrigerator for 30 minutes.

3. Place your hand over the grate to test the heat in each section. Place the kebabs over medium heat—a spot you can leave your hand over for 5 seconds before you need to move it away. Grill the kebabs until they are charred all over and cooked through, 10 to 12 minutes, turning them as little as necessary.

4. Remove the kebabs from heat and let them rest for 2 minutes before serving.

Yield: 4 to 6 Servings

Total Time: 3 Hours

CARNE ASADA

1 jalapeño chile pepper, stem and seeds removed, minced

3 garlic cloves, minced

½ cup chopped fresh cilantro

¼ cup avocado oil

Juice of 1 orange

2 tablespoons apple cider vinegar

2 teaspoons cayenne pepper

1 teaspoon ancho chile powder

1 teaspoon garlic powder

1 teaspoon paprika

1 teaspoon kosher salt

1 teaspoon cumin

1 teaspoon dried oregano

¼ teaspoon black pepper

2 lbs. flank steak, trimmed

1. Place all of the ingredients, except for the steak, in a large resealable plastic bag and stir to combine. Add the steak, place the bag in the refrigerator, and let the steak marinate for 2 hours.

2. Prepare a fire, either setting up an even coal bed if you are able to adjust the height of your grate easily, or banking the coals to set up one zone for direct heat and another for indirect. Set up a grate over the coals.

3. Remove the steak from the marinade, pat it dry, and let it rest at room temperature.

4. Place your hand over the grate to test the heat in each section. Place the steak over medium-high heat—a spot you can leave your hand over for 3 or 4 seconds before you need to move it away. Grill until the steak is medium-rare (the interior reads 130°F on an instant-read thermometer) and the exterior is nicely seared, 6 to 8 minutes, turning it over just once.

5. Remove the steak from heat and let it rest for 2 minutes before slicing it thin against the grain and serving.

Yield: 4 Servings

Total Time: 4 Hours and 30 Minutes

BRAISED SHORT RIBS

4 lbs. short ribs

Salt and pepper, to taste

2 tablespoons extra-virgin olive oil

2 large onions, sliced

4 carrots, peeled and diced

4 large potatoes, peeled and diced

8 cups Beef Stock (see page 249)

4 bay leaves

½ cup red wine

1 tablespoon chopped fresh rosemary

1 teaspoon fresh thyme

1. Prepare a fire, either setting up an even coal bed if you are able to adjust the height of your grate easily, or banking the coals to set up one zone for direct heat and another for indirect. Set up a grate over the coals.

2. Generously season the short ribs with salt. Place your hand over the grate to test the heat in each section. Place the short ribs over medium heat—a spot you can leave your hand over for 5 seconds before you need to move it away. Cook until the short ribs are browned all over, about 5 minutes, turning them as necessary. Remove the short ribs from the grill and set them aside.

3. Place a Dutch oven over medium-high heat—a spot you can leave your hand over for 3 or 4 seconds before you need to move it away—and add the olive oil. Add the onions, carrots, and potatoes and cook, stirring occasionally, until the onions start to soften, about 5 minutes.

4. Add the stock, bay leaves, and short ribs to the pot, and cover it. Carefully nestle the Dutch oven into the coal bed and cook the short ribs until the meat easily comes away from the bone, about 4 hours.

5. Carefully remove the Dutch oven from the coals. Stir the red wine, rosemary, and thyme into the Dutch oven and place it over medium heat. Cook until the liquid has reduced, about 10 minutes.

6. Season the dish with salt and pepper. To serve, divide the short ribs and vegetables among the serving plates and ladle 2 to 3 tablespoons of the sauce over each portion.

BEEF SHAWARMA

3 lbs. top sirloin

6 tablespoons extra-virgin olive oil

3 tablespoons red wine vinegar

Juice of 2 lemons

2 teaspoons cinnamon

2 tablespoons coriander

1 tablespoon black pepper

1 teaspoon cardamom

1 teaspoon ground cloves

½ teaspoon mace

⅛ teaspoon freshly grated nutmeg

1 tablespoon garlic powder

2 yellow onions, sliced into thin half-moons

Salt, to taste

1 teaspoon sumac

1 cup full-fat Greek yogurt, for serving

Pita Bread (see page 191), for serving

2 Persian cucumbers, diced, for serving

2 Roma tomatoes, diced, for serving

½ cup fresh mint or parsley, torn, for serving

1. Place the olive oil, vinegar, lemon juice, cinnamon, coriander, pepper, cardamom, cloves, mace, nutmeg, and garlic powder in a mixing bowl and stir to combine. Place the steak in a baking dish, pour the marinade over it, and place it in the refrigerator. Let the steak marinate for 1 hour.

2. Place the sliced onions in a baking dish and cover them with water. Add a pinch of salt and several ice cubes. Place the onions in the refrigerator and chill for 30 minutes.

3. Prepare a fire, either setting up an even coal bed if you are able to adjust the height of your grate easily, or banking the coals to set up one zone for direct heat and another for indirect. Set up a grate over the coals.

4. Remove the steak and onions from the refrigerator. Let the meat sit at room temperature. Drain the onions, squeeze them to remove any excess water, and place them in a bowl. Add the sumac and toss to coat. Set the onions aside.

5. Place your hand over the grate to test the heat in each section. Place the steak over medium-high heat—a spot you can leave your hand over for 3 or 4 seconds before you need to move it away. Cook until the steak is medium-rare (the interior reads 130°F on an instant-read thermometer) and the exterior is nicely seared, 8 to 10 minutes.

6. Remove the steak from heat and let it rest for 2 minutes before slicing it thin against the grain. To serve, place a dollop of yogurt on a pita and top with some of the meat, onions, cucumbers, tomatoes, and mint or parsley.

Yield: 6 Servings

Total Time: 2 Hours

LAMB SHARBA

¾ lb. boneless leg of lamb, cut into 1-inch cubes

2 tablespoons extra-virgin olive oil

1 onion, chopped

1 tomato, quartered, deseeded, and sliced thin

1 garlic clove, minced

1 tablespoon tomato paste

1 bunch of fresh mint, tied with twine, plus more for garnish

2 cinnamon sticks

1¼ teaspoons turmeric

1¼ teaspoons paprika

½ teaspoons cumin

8 cups Chicken Stock (see page 245)

1 (14 oz.) can of chickpeas, drained and rinsed

¾ cup orzo

Salt and pepper, to taste

1. Prepare a fire, either setting up an even coal bed if you are able to adjust the height of your grate easily, or banking the coals to set up one zone for direct heat and another for indirect. Set up a grate over the coals.

2. Place your hand over the grate to test the heat in each section. Place the lamb over medium-high heat—a spot you can leave your hand over for 3 or 4 seconds before you need to move it away. Cook until the lamb is seared all over, about 5 minutes, turning it as necessary. Remove the lamb from heat and set it aside.

3. Place half of the olive oil in a Dutch oven and place it over medium-high heat. Add the onion to the pot and cook, stirring occasionally, until it starts to soften, about 5 minutes. Add the tomato, garlic, tomato paste, mint, cinnamon sticks, turmeric, paprika, and cumin and cook, stirring continually, for 1 minute.

4. Add the stock and bring the mixture to a boil. Add the seared lamb to the pot, cover it, and carefully nestle it down into the coal bed. Cook the stew until the lamb is tender, about 30 minutes.

5. Carefully remove the Dutch oven's cover and add the chickpeas and orzo. Cover the Dutch oven and cook the stew until the orzo is tender, about 10 minutes.

6. Carefully remove the Dutch oven from the coals and remove the cover. Remove the mint from the stew and discard it.

7. Season the stew with salt and pepper and ladle it into warmed bowls. Garnish with additional mint and enjoy.

Yield: 4 Servings

Total Time: 1 Hour

SPICY LAMB CHOPS WITH RAITA

4 bone-in lamb chops, each about 1 inch thick

2 tablespoons extra-virgin olive oil

Kashmiri Chile Rub (see page 201)

Raita (see page 148), for serving

I. Rub the lamb chops with the olive oil and then generously apply the rub, making sure both sides are coated. Let the lamb chops rest at room temperature.

2. Prepare a fire, either setting up an even coal bed if you are able to adjust the height of your grate easily, or banking the coals to set up one zone for direct heat and another for indirect. Set up a grate over the coals.

3. Place your hand over the grate to test the heat in each section. Place the lamb chops over medium-low heat—a spot you can leave your hand over for 6 or 7 seconds before you need to move it away. Cook until the lamb chops are medium-rare (the interior reads 125°F on an instant-read thermometer) and the exteriors are nicely seared, 17 to 20 minutes, turning them over just once.

4. Remove the lamb chops from heat and let them rest for 3 minutes before serving with the Raita.

ROSEMARY & LEMON LEG OF LAMB

¾ cup extra-virgin olive oil

¼ cup fresh rosemary, chopped

Juice of 3 lemons

4 garlic cloves, minced

4 lb. boneless leg of lamb, butterflied

Salt and pepper, to taste

1. Place the olive oil, rosemary, lemon juice, and garlic in a mixing bowl and mix thoroughly.

2. Season the lamb generously with salt and pepper and place it in a roasting pan. Pour the marinade over the lamb and let it marinate in the refrigerator overnight.

3. Prepare a fire, either setting up an even coal bed if you are able to adjust the height of your grate easily, or banking the coals to set up one zone for direct heat and another for indirect. Set up a grate over the coals.

4. Remove the lamb from the refrigerator and let it rest at room temperature.

5. Place your hand over the grate to test the heat in each section. Place the lamb over medium heat—a spot you can leave your hand over for 5 seconds before you need to move it away. Cook until the lamb is medium-rare (the interior reads 125°F on an instant-read thermometer) and the exterior is nicely seared, 30 to 35 minutes, turning it over just once.

6. Remove the lamb from heat and let it rest for 5 minutes before slicing and serving.

Yield: 6 Servings

Total Time: 3 Hours and 30 Minutes

GRILLED LAMB LOIN WITH CHIMICHURRI

2½ lb. lamb tenderloin, trimmed

Lamb Marinade (see page 212)

Chimichurri Sauce (see page 237), for serving

1. Rub the lamb with the marinade and marinate it in the refrigerator for at least 2 hours.

2. Prepare a fire, either setting up an even coal bed if you are able to adjust the height of your grate easily, or banking the coals to set up one zone for direct heat and another for indirect. Set up a grate over the coals.

3. Place your hand over the grate to test the heat in each section. Place the lamb over medium-high heat—a spot you can leave your hand over for 3 or 4 seconds before you need to move it away. Cook until the interior of the lamb registers 140°F on an instant-read thermometer and the exterior is nicely seared, 15 to 20 minutes, turning it as little as possible.

4. Remove the lamb from the grill and let it rest for 10 minutes before slicing and serving with the Chimichurri Sauce.

ROGAN JOSH

2 lbs. boneless lamb shoulder, cut into 1-inch pieces

Salt, to taste

3 tablespoons olive oil

2 large yellow onions, sliced thin

2-inch piece of fresh ginger, peeled and minced

2 garlic cloves, minced

1 tablespoon curry powder, plus 1 teaspoon

1 teaspoon turmeric

1 teaspoon cayenne pepper, or to taste

1 teaspoon garam masala

1 (14 oz.) can of crushed tomatoes

1 cup plain yogurt

2 cups water

Fresh cilantro, finely chopped, for garnish

Red onion, minced, for garnish

1. Prepare a fire, either setting up an even coal bed if you are able to adjust the height of your grate easily, or banking the coals to set up one zone for direct heat and another for indirect. Set up a grate over the coals.

2. Generously season the lamb with salt. Place your hand over the grate to test the heat in each section. Place the lamb over medium heat—a spot you can leave your hand over for 5 seconds before you need to move it away. Cook until the lamb is browned all over, about 5 minutes, turning it as necessary. Remove the lamb from the grill and set it aside.

3. Place a Dutch oven over medium-high heat—a spot you can leave your hand over for 3 or 4 seconds before you need to move it away—and add the olive oil. Add the onion and cook, stirring occasionally, until it has softened, about 5 minutes. Add the ginger, garlic, curry powder, turmeric, cayenne, and garam masala and cook, stirring continually, for 1 minute.

4. Add the tomatoes, yogurt, and water to the Dutch oven and bring to a gentle boil. Add the lamb to the pot and cover it. Carefully nestle the Dutch oven into the coal bed and cook until the lamb is very tender, about 1 hour.

5. Ladle the rogan josh into warmed bowls, garnish with the cilantro and red onion, and enjoy.

LAMB KEBABS

1½ lbs. ground lamb

1 onion, grated

1 teaspoon chopped fresh rosemary

3 garlic cloves, minced

1 teaspoon cumin

½ teaspoon dried thyme

Salt and pepper, to taste

Pita Bread (see page 191), for serving

Full-fat Greek yogurt, for serving

I. Prepare a fire, either setting up an even coal bed if you are able to adjust the height of your grate easily, or banking the coals to set up one zone for direct heat and another for indirect. Set up a grate over the coals. If using bamboo skewers, soak them in water.

2. Place all of the ingredients in a mixing bowl and work the mixture with your hands until well combined. Form the meat into an oblong shape around the skewers and chill them in the refrigerator for 30 minutes.

3. Place your hand over the grate to test the heat in each section. Place the kebabs over medium heat—a spot you can leave your hand over for 5 seconds before you need to move it away. Grill the kebabs until they are charred all over and cooked through, 10 to 12 minutes, turning them as little as necessary.

4. Remove the kebabs from heat and let them rest for 2 minutes before serving with Pita Bread and yogurt.

POTJIEKOS

¼ cup extra-virgin olive oil

4 large yellow onions, chopped

4 teaspoons curry powder

Zest and juice of 1 orange

2 red chile peppers, stems and seeds removed, chopped

4 curry leaves

4 bay leaves

2 lbs. lamb shank, cubed

1 large white yam, peeled and chopped

1 large sweet potato, peeled and chopped

2 large potatoes, peeled and chopped

4 large carrots, peeled and chopped

4 large garlic cloves

2 cups fresh spinach, stemmed

Salt, to taste

1. Prepare a fire, either setting up an even coal bed if you are able to adjust the height of your grate easily, or banking the coals to set up one zone for direct heat and another for indirect. Set up a grate over the coals.

2. Place your hand over the grate to test the heat in each section. Place the olive oil in a Dutch oven and place it over medium-high heat—a spot you can leave your hand over for 3 or 4 seconds before you need to move it away. Add the onions and cook, stirring occasionally, until they are lightly browned, about 5 minutes.

3. Add the curry powder, orange zest, chiles, curry leaves, bay leaves, and lamb and cook, stirring occasionally, until the lamb is browned all over, about 10 minutes.

4. Add the orange juice and enough water to cover the contents of the pot. Layer the yam, sweet potato, potatoes, carrots, and garlic on top. Cover the Dutch oven, remove it from the grill, and carefully nestle it down into the coal bed. Let the stew cook until the lamb is very tender, 2 to 3 hours.

5. Carefully remove the Dutch oven from the coals. Stir in the spinach and season the stew with salt. Ladle the stew into warmed bowls and enjoy.

POULTRY & PORK

Chicken, though lighter than beef and lamb, becomes no less exceptional over the flame. And pork, which is always obliging to a low-and-slow approach, supplies invaluable instruction and unmatched comfort in each and every preparation.

Yield: 4 Servings

Total Time: 24 Hours

PERI-PERI CHICKEN

2 lbs. bone-in, skin-on chicken legs

Peri-Peri Marinade (see page 214)

Lime wedges, for serving

1. Place the chicken in a baking dish and rub it with half of the marinade. Let the chicken marinate in the refrigerator overnight. Store the remaining marinade in the refrigerator.

2. Prepare a fire, either setting up an even coal bed if you are able to adjust the height of your grate easily, or banking the coals to set up one zone for direct heat and another for indirect. Set up a grate over the coals.

3. Remove the chicken from the marinade. Place your hand over the grate to test the heat in each section. Place the chicken over medium heat—a spot you can leave your hand over for 5 seconds before you need to move it away. Cook until the interior of the chicken registers 165°F on an instant-read thermometer and the skin is nice and crispy, 25 to 30 minutes, turning it as little as possible.

4. Remove the chicken from heat and brush it with the remaining marinade. Serve with lime wedges and enjoy.

Yield: 6 Servings

Total Time: 40 Minutes

CHICKEN TAGINE

8 bone-in, skin-on chicken drumsticks or thighs

Salt and pepper, to taste

2 tablespoons extra-virgin olive oil

1 onion, minced

4 garlic cloves, minced

1 teaspoon grated fresh ginger

Zest of 1 lemon

1 teaspoon paprika

½ teaspoon cumin

⅛ teaspoon cayenne pepper

½ teaspoon coriander

¼ teaspoon cinnamon

½ cup white wine

2 cups Chicken Stock (see page 245)

1 carrot, peeled and cut into thin half-moons

1 tablespoon honey

¾ cup halved dried apricots

1 (14 oz.) can of chickpeas, drained and rinsed

Fresh mint, chopped, for garnish

Israeli couscous, cooked, for serving

1. Prepare a fire, either setting up an even coal bed if you are able to adjust the height of your grate easily, or banking the coals to set up one zone for direct heat and another for indirect. Set up a grate over the coals.

2. Season the chicken with salt and pepper. Place your hand over the grate to test the heat in each section. Place the chicken over medium-high heat—a spot you can leave your hand over for 3 or 4 seconds before you need to move it away. Cook until the skin is golden brown, 5 to 7 minutes, turning the chicken as necessary. Remove the chicken from heat and set it aside.

3. Place a Dutch oven over medium-high heat and add the olive oil. Add the onion, and cook, stirring occasionally, until it has softened, about 5 minutes. Add the garlic, ginger, lemon zest, paprika, cumin, cayenne, coriander, and cinnamon and cook, stirring continually, for 1 minute.

4. Add the white wine and cook for 3 minutes, scraping up any browned bits from the bottom of the pot.

5. Add the stock, carrot, honey, and apricots and bring the mixture to a simmer. Add the chickpeas, nestle the chicken into the mixture, and cover the Dutch oven. Carefully nestle it into the coal bed and cook until the chicken is cooked through, about 25 to 30 minutes.

6. Carefully remove the tagine from the coals. Garnish it with mint, serve with couscous, and enjoy.

Yield: 4 Servings

Total Time: 24 Hours

JAMAICAN JERK CHICKEN

8 bone-in, skin-on chicken thighs

Jerk Marinade (see page 208)

Grilled pineapple, for serving

1. Place the chicken in a baking dish and pour the marinade over it. Let the chicken marinate in the refrigerator overnight.

2. Prepare a fire, either setting up an even coal bed if you are able to adjust the height of your grate easily, or banking the coals to set up one zone for direct heat and another for indirect. Set up a grate over the coals.

3. Remove the chicken from the marinade and let it rest at room temperature.

4. Place your hand over the grate to test the heat in each section. Place the chicken, skin side down, over medium heat—a spot you can leave your hand over for 5 seconds before you need to move it away. Cook until the interior of the chicken reads 165°F on an instant-read thermometer and the skin is nice and crispy, 20 to 25 minutes, turning them over just once.

5. Remove the chicken from the grill and let it rest for 2 minutes before serving alongside grilled pineapple.

Yield: 4 to 6 Servings

Total Time: 2½ Hours

CHICKEN KEBABS

2 tablespoons paprika

1 teaspoon turmeric

1 teaspoon onion powder

1 teaspoon garlic powder

1 tablespoon dried oregano

¼ cup extra-virgin olive oil

2 tablespoons white wine vinegar

1 cup full-fat Greek yogurt

1 teaspoon kosher salt, plus more to taste

2 lbs. boneless, skinless chicken thighs, cubed

Black pepper, to taste

Lemon wedges, for serving

1. Place the paprika, turmeric, onion powder, garlic powder, oregano, olive oil, vinegar, yogurt, and salt in a large bowl and whisk to combine.

2. Add the chicken and stir until it is coated. Let the chicken marinate in the refrigerator for 2 hours.

3. Prepare a fire, either setting up an even coal bed if you are able to adjust the height of your grate easily, or banking the coals to set up one zone for direct heat and another for indirect. Set up a grate over the coals. If using bamboo skewers, soak them in water.

4. Remove the chicken from the marinade, thread it onto skewers, and season it with salt and pepper.

5. Place your hand over the grate to test the heat in each section. Place the skewers over medium heat—a spot you can leave your hand over for 5 seconds before you need to move it away. Grill until the chicken is cooked through and charred, about 15 minutes, turning them as little as possible.

6. Remove the skewers from heat, let them rest for 2 minutes, and serve with lemon wedges.

CHICKEN KEBABS

See page 73

SLOW-COOKED MOLASSES BBQ RIBS

5 lbs. pork ribs

½ cup kosher salt

2 tablespoons light brown sugar

2 tablespoons garlic powder

1 tablespoon onion powder

1 tablespoon chili powder

1 tablespoon paprika

1 tablespoon cumin

Molasses BBQ Sauce
(see page 230)

1. If your butcher has not already done so, remove the thin membrane from the back of each rack of ribs. Place the ribs in a roasting pan. Place all of the remaining ingredients, except for the Molasses BBQ Sauce, in a bowl and stir until combined. Rub the mixture in the bowl all over the ribs, making sure every inch is covered. Place the ribs in the refrigerator for 1 hour.

2. Prepare a fire, either setting up an even coal bed if you are able to adjust the height of your grate easily, or banking the coals to set up one zone for direct heat and another for indirect. Set up a grate over the coals.

3. Place 2 to 3 layers of heavy-duty aluminum foil down, place the ribs on the foil, and securely wrap the ribs, making sure there are no holes or tears in the foil. Crimp the edges of the packet to seal.

4. Place your hand over the grate to test the heat in each section. Place the ribs over low heat—a spot you can comfortably leave your hand over for 9 seconds. Cook until the ribs begin to pull away from the bones, 3 to 4 hours, brushing them with some of the BBQ sauce every 20 or 30 minutes.

5. Remove the ribs from the foil packet and place them over medium-high heat—a spot you can leave your hand over for 3 or 4 seconds before you need to move it away. Cook the ribs until they have caramelized.

6. Remove the ribs from heat and let them rest for 20 minutes before serving.

Yield: 4 Servings

Total Time: 1 Hour and 15 Minutes

BROWN SUGAR RIBS

2 racks of baby back pork ribs

2 cups brown sugar

2 tablespoons kosher salt

2 tablespoons freshly ground black pepper

2 tablespoons ancho chile powder (optional)

1 lb. bacon fat, chilled or at room temperature

BBQ sauce, for serving

1. Prepare a fire, either setting up an even coal bed if you are able to adjust the height of your grate easily, or banking the coals to set up one zone for direct heat and another for indirect. Set up a grate over the coals.

2. If your butcher has not already done so, remove the thin membrane from the back of each rack of ribs.

3. Place the brown sugar, salt, pepper, and chile powder in a bowl and stir to combine. Generously rub the mixture over the ribs, and then coat the ribs with the bacon fat. Place 2 to 3 layers of heavy-duty aluminum foil down, place the racks of ribs, side by side, on top of the foil, and securely wrap the ribs, making sure there are no holes or tears in the foil. Crimp the edges of the packet to seal.

4. Place your hand over the grate to test the heat in each section. Place the ribs over medium heat—a spot you can leave your hand over for 5 seconds before you need to move it away. Cook until the ribs begin to pull away from the bones, 45 minutes to 1 hour.

5. Remove the ribs from the foil packet and place them over medium-high heat—a spot you can leave your hand over for 3 or 4 seconds before you need to move it away. Cook the ribs until they are lightly charred on each side.

6. Remove the ribs from the grill and serve with your favorite BBQ sauce.

Yield: 4 Servings

Total Time: 1 Hour

CHICKEN TERIYAKI BURGERS

---

1 lb. ground chicken

½ teaspoon white pepper

1 egg white

1 tablespoon teriyaki sauce

4 pineapple rings, each about ½-inch thick

Hamburger buns, for serving

1. Prepare a fire, either setting up an even coal bed if you are able to adjust the height of your grate easily, or banking the coals to set up one zone for direct heat and another for indirect. Set up a grate over the coals.

2. Place all of the ingredients, except for the pineapple, in a mixing bowl and work the mixture until well combined. Divide the mixture into four equal parts and form each one into a 1-inch-thick patty.

3. Place your hand over the grate to test the heat in each section. Place the burgers over medium-high heat—a spot you can leave your hand over for 3 or 4 seconds before you need to move it away. Cook for 5 minutes.

4. Place the pineapple over medium-high heat and cook until it is charred on both sides, about 5 minutes.

5. Flip the burgers over and cook until they are cooked through, 5 to 6 minutes.

6. Remove the pineapple and burgers from heat, top the burgers with the charred pineapple, and serve with hamburger buns.

Yield: 4 Servings

Total Time: 2 Hours and 30 Minutes

CHICKEN SOUVLAKI

10 garlic cloves, crushed

4 sprigs of fresh oregano

1 sprig of fresh rosemary

1 teaspoon paprika

1 teaspoon kosher salt

1 teaspoon black pepper

¼ cup extra-virgin olive oil, plus more as needed

¼ cup dry white wine

2 tablespoons fresh lemon juice

2½ lbs. boneless, skinless chicken thighs, chopped

2 bay leaves

Pita Bread (see page 191), warmed, for serving

1. Place the garlic, oregano, rosemary, paprika, salt, pepper, olive oil, wine, and lemon juice in a food processor and blitz to combine.

2. Place the chicken and bay leaves in a bowl or a large resealable bag, pour the marinade over the chicken, and marinate in the refrigerator for 2 hours.

3. Prepare a fire, either setting up an even coal bed if you are able to adjust the height of your grate easily, or banking the coals to set up one zone for direct heat and another for indirect. Set up a grate over the coals. If using bamboo skewers, soak them in water.

4. Remove the chicken from the marinade and thread it onto the skewers.

5. Place your hand over the grate to test the heat in each section. Place the chicken over medium heat—a spot you can leave your hand over for 5 seconds before you need to move it away. Cook until the chicken is cooked through and the exterior is lightly charred, about 15 minutes, turning it as little as possible.

6. Remove the skewers from heat and let them rest for 2 minutes. Serve with pita and vegetables and herbs of your choice and enjoy.

CHICKEN SOUVLAKI

See page 81

Yield: 5 to 10 Servings

Total Time: 2½ to 3 Hours

SPATCHCOCK TURKEY

2 teaspoons kosher salt

2 teaspoons black pepper

1 tablespoon garlic powder

1 tablespoon onion powder

10 to 20 lb. turkey, giblets and innards removed

5 tablespoons unsalted butter, melted

I. Place the salt, pepper, garlic powder, and onion powder in a bowl and stir to combine. Set the mixture aside.

2. Place the turkey on a cutting board, breast side down. Using kitchen shears, cut out the backbone of the turkey.

3. Flip the turkey back over so the breast side is up and set it on a wire rack placed inside a roasting pan. Push down on the middle of the bird to flatten it as much as possible.

4. Rub the melted butter all over the breast side of the turkey and then rub the salt mixture all over the breast side of the turkey. Place the turkey in the refrigerator.

5. Prepare a fire, either setting up an even coal bed if you are able to adjust the height of your grate easily, or banking the coals to set up one zone for direct heat and another for indirect. Set up a grate over the coals.

6. Place your hand over the grate to test the heat in each section. Place the turkey, breast side down, over medium-low heat—a spot you can leave your hand over for 6 or 7 seconds before you need to move it away. Cook until the interior of the thickest part of the turkey's leg registers 165°F on an instant-read thermometer and the skin is nice and crispy, turning it just once. The cooking time will depend on the size of the turkey, but plan for anywhere from 1 hour and 15 minutes to 1 hour and 45 minutes.

7. Remove the turkey from heat and let it rest for 20 minutes before slicing and serving.

ROTISSERIE CHICKEN

Poultry Brine (see page 209)

4 lb. whole chicken

1. Place the brine in a large stockpot and add the chicken. You want to ensure that the entire bird is submerged. If it is not, weigh the chicken down with a few plates. Brine the chicken in the refrigerator overnight.

2. Prepare a fire, setting up an even coal bed. Set up a rotisserie over the coals.

3. Remove the chicken from the marinade and thread it onto the rotisserie. Cook the chicken until the drumstick breaks away from the bone at the end when you pull up on it or an instant-read thermometer registers 160°F when inserted into the thickest part of the thigh.

4. Remove the chicken from heat and let it rest for 10 minutes before carving. This period of rest should bring the temperature of the interior up to 165°F.

Yield: 4 Servings

Total Time: 24 Hours

SPATCHCOCK ZA'ATAR CHICKEN

4 lb. whole chicken

2 tablespoons extra-virgin olive oil

¼ cup Za'atar (see page 205)

1. Place a wire rack in a rimmed baking sheet. Place the chicken, breast side down, on a cutting board. Using kitchen shears, cut out the chicken's backbone. Flip the chicken over so the breast side is facing up. Push down on the middle of the chicken to flatten it as much as possible. Pat the chicken dry and place it on the wire rack.

2. Place the chicken in the refrigerator and let it rest, uncovered, overnight.

3. Remove the chicken from the refrigerator and rub it with the olive oil. Sprinkle the Za'atar over the chicken and let it rest at room temperature for 30 minutes.

4. Prepare a fire, either setting up an even coal bed if you are able to adjust the height of your grate easily, or banking the coals to set up one zone for direct heat and another for indirect. Set up a grate over the coals.

5. Place your hand over the grate to test the heat in each section. Place the chicken, breast side down, over medium heat—a spot you can leave your hand over for 5 seconds before you need to move it away. Cook until the chicken is very crispy, about 10 minutes. Turn the chicken over and cook until the interior of the thickest part of the thigh is 165°F on an instant-read thermometer.

6. Remove the chicken from heat and let it rest for 5 minutes before serving.

DWAEJI BULGOGI

2 lbs. pork tenderloin

4 garlic cloves, minced

1 tablespoon grated
fresh ginger

½ cup gochujang

2 tablespoons soy sauce

3 tablespoons sesame oil

Sesame seeds, for garnish

2 scallions, trimmed and
chopped, for garnish

White rice, cooked,
for serving

Romaine lettuce leaves,
for serving

Musaengchae (see page 154),
for serving

1. Place all of the ingredients, except for the pork and those designated for garnish or for serving, in a bowl and stir to combine. Place the pork in a baking dish, pour the marinade over it, and let the meat marinate in the refrigerator for 1 hour.

2. Prepare a fire, either setting up an even coal bed if you are able to adjust the height of your grate easily, or banking the coals to set up one zone for direct heat and another for indirect. Set up a grate over the coals.

3. Remove the pork from the marinade. Place your hand over the grate to test the heat in each section. Place the pork over medium-high heat—a spot you can leave your hand over for 3 or 4 seconds before you need to move it away. Grill until the interior of the pork registers 145°F on an instant-read thermometer and the exterior is nicely seared, 15 to 20 minutes.

4. Remove the pork from heat and let it rest for 5 minutes.

5. Slice the pork thin and garnish it with the sesame seeds and scallions. Serve with white rice, romaine lettuce leaves, and Musaengchae and enjoy.

SPICY ORANGE PORK

3 tablespoons extra-virgin olive oil

1½ cups fresh orange juice, strained

2 teaspoons orange zest

1 garlic clove, chopped

2 bay leaves

Pinch of chili powder

Pinch of dried oregano

2½ lb. pork tenderloin

Salt and pepper, to taste

1. Prepare a fire, either setting up an even coal bed if you are able to adjust the height of your grate easily, or banking the coals to set up one zone for direct heat and another for indirect. Set up a grate over the coals.

2. Place your hand over the grate to test the heat in each section. Place the olive oil in a large cast-iron skillet and place it over medium-high heat—a spot you can leave your hand over for 3 or 4 seconds before you need to move it away. Gently pour the fresh orange juice into the pan and then stir in the orange zest, garlic, bay leaves, chili powder, and oregano. Let the mixture come to a simmer.

3. Season the pork with salt and pepper and place it in the pan. Braise the pork until it registers 135°F on an instant-read thermometer, abut 1½ hours, basting it occasionally.

4. Remove the pork from the pan and place it directly on the grate. Cook until the pork registers 145°F on an instant-read thermometer and the exterior is nicely seared, about 10 minutes, turning it as necessary.

5. Remove the pork from the grill and let it rest for 5 minutes before slicing and serving.

Yield: 4 Servings

Total Time: 2 Hours

SPLIT PEA SOUP WITH SMOKED HAM

2 tablespoons unsalted butter

1 onion, minced

1 carrot, peeled and minced

1 celery stalk, minced

5 cups Chicken Stock
(see page 245)

1 cup yellow split peas

½ lb. smoked ham, chopped

2 tablespoons chopped fresh
parsley, plus more for garnish

1 bay leaf

1 teaspoon fresh thyme

Salt and pepper, to taste

Lemon wedges, for serving

1. Prepare a fire, either setting up an even coal bed if you are able to adjust the height of your grate easily, or banking the coals to set up one zone for direct heat and another for indirect. Set up a grate over the coals.

2. Place your hand over the grate to test the heat in each section. Place a Dutch oven over medium heat—a spot you can leave your hand over for 5 seconds before you need to move it away—and add the butter. Add the onion, carrot, and celery and cook, stirring frequently, until they have softened, about 5 minutes.

3. Add the stock, split peas, ham, parsley, bay leaf, and thyme. Bring the soup to a boil and then move the Dutch oven over medium-low heat— a spot you can leave your hand over for 6 or 7 seconds before you need to move it away. Simmer, stirring occasionally, until the peas are al dente, about 1 hour.

4. Remove the bay leaf from the soup and discard it. Season the soup with salt and pepper and ladle it into warmed bowls. Garnish with additional parsley and serve with lemon wedges.

Yield: 4 Servings

Total Time: 1 Hour and 30 Minutes

PORK & APPLE CASSEROLE

8 apples, cored and sliced

2 teaspoons cinnamon

1 teaspoon grated fresh nutmeg

¼ cup sugar

¼ cup all-purpose flour

Salt and pepper, to taste

¼ cup apple cider

1½ lb. pork tenderloin

2 tablespoons ground fresh rosemary

2 tablespoons ground fresh thyme

1. Prepare a fire, piling the coals in a large mound.

2. Place the apples, cinnamon, nutmeg, sugar, flour, and a pinch of salt in a mixing bowl and stir to combine. Transfer the mixture to a Dutch oven and then stir in the apple cider.

3. Rub the pork with the ground herbs and a pinch of salt. Place the pork on top of the apple mixture and cover the Dutch oven.

4. Carefully nestle the Dutch oven into the coal bed and cook until the center of the pork registers 145°F, about 1 to 1½ hours.

5. Carefully remove the Dutch oven from the coal bed. Remove the pork tenderloin from the pot and let it rest for 10 minutes before slicing it thin and serving it on beds of the apple mixture.

PORCHETTA

5 to 6 lb. skin-on pork belly

1 tablespoon finely chopped fresh rosemary

1 tablespoon fresh thyme

1 tablespoon chopped fresh sage

2 teaspoons garlic powder

Salt, to taste

1-lb. center-cut pork tenderloin

1. Place the pork belly skin side down on a cutting board. Using a sharp knife, score the flesh in a crosshatch pattern, cutting about ¼ inch deep. Flip the pork belly over and poke small holes in the skin. Turn the pork belly back over and rub the minced herbs, garlic powder, and salt into the scored flesh. Place the pork tenderloin in the center of the pork belly and then roll the pork belly up so that it retains its length. Tie the rolled pork belly securely with kitchen twine every ½ inch.

2. Transfer the porchetta to a rack set in a large roasting pan, place it in the fridge, and leave it uncovered for 2 days. This allows the skin to dry out a bit. Blot the porchetta occasionally with paper towels to remove excess moisture.

3. Remove the porchetta from the refrigerator and let it stand at room temperature.

4. Prepare a fire, either setting up an even coal bed if you are able to adjust the height of your grate easily, or banking the coals to set up one zone for direct heat and another for indirect. Set up a grate over the coals.

5. Place your hand over the grate to test the heat in each section. Place the porchetta over medium-high heat—a spot you can leave your hand over for 3 or 4 seconds before you need to move it away. Cook until the exterior is seared all over, 8 to 10 minutes, turning the porchetta as needed.

6. Move the porchetta over medium-low heat—a spot you can leave your hand over for 6 or 7 seconds before you need to move it away. Cook the porchetta until the center is 145°F on an instant-read thermometer, 1 to 2 hours, turning it as little as possible.

7. Remove the porchetta from heat and let it rest for 15 minutes before slicing and serving.

Yield: 4 Servings

Total Time: 1 Hour

PORK CHOPS

4 bone-in pork chops, each
1 to 1½ inches thick

Salt and pepper, to taste

1. Prepare a fire, either setting up an even coal bed if you are able to adjust the height of your grate easily, or banking the coals to set up one zone for direct heat and another for indirect. Set up a grate over the coals.

2. Season the pork chops with salt and pepper. Place your hand over the grate to test the heat in each section. Place the pork chops over medium heat—a spot you can leave your hand over for 5 seconds before you need to move it away. Cook until the center of the pork chops are 145°F on an instant-read thermometer and the exteriors are nicely seared, 10 to 12 minutes.

3. Remove the pork chops from heat and let them rest for 2 minutes before serving.

PORK CHOPS

See page 99

Yield: 6 Servings

Total Time: 4 Hours and 30 Minutes

CARNITAS

1 tablespoon fresh lime juice

2 teaspoons kosher salt

2 teaspoons cumin

1 teaspoon chili powder

2 teaspoons Tajín

1 teaspoon Mexican oregano

1 teaspoon garlic powder

1 teaspoon onion powder

1 teaspoon black pepper

¼ cup lard

3 lbs. boneless pork shoulder, trimmed and cut into cubes

Salsa, for serving

Fresh cilantro, chopped, for serving

Lime wedges, for serving

Corn Tortillas (see page 180), for serving

1. Place the lime juice, salt, cumin, chili powder, Tajín, oregano, garlic powder, onion powder, and pepper in a bowl and stir to combine. Set the mixture aside.

2. Prepare a fire, either setting up an even coal bed if you are able to adjust the height of your grate easily, or banking the coals to set up one zone for direct heat and another for indirect. Set up a grate over the coals.

3. Place your hand over the grate to test the heat in each section. Place a Dutch oven over medium-high heat—a spot you can leave your hand over for 3 or 4 seconds before you need to move it away—and add the lard. Working in batches to avoid crowding the pot, add the pork and cook until it is browned all over, turning it as necessary.

4. Add all of the pork to the Dutch oven, pour the seasoning mixture over it, and cover the Dutch oven. Move the Dutch oven over medium-low heat—a a spot you can leave your hand over for 6 or 7 seconds before you need to move it away. Cook the pork until it is extremely tender, 3 to 4 hours.

5. Remove the Dutch oven from heat and shred the pork. Serve with salsa, cilantro, lime wedges, and Corn Tortillas.

SEAFOOD

Seafood is a natural for the grill, with mildly flavored flesh that eagerly embraces smoke, and a lean character that cooks quickly. These attributes also mean that seafood requires more care, but do not worry—the thorough instructions in this section will teach you how to remain on the right side of the line when handling the delicate fruits of the sea.

Yield: 6 Servings

Total Time: 1 Hour

BLACKENED SALMON

2 lbs. salmon fillets, skin removed

¼ cup Blackening Spice (see page 204)

Zest of 1 lemon

Lemon wedges, for serving

1. Prepare a fire, either setting up an even coal bed if you are able to adjust the height of your grate easily, or banking the coals to set up one zone for direct heat and another for indirect. Set up a grate over the coals.

2. Rub the salmon with the Blackening Spice. Place your hand over the grate to test the heat in each section. Place the salmon over high heat—a spot you can only leave your hand over for 2 seconds before you need to move it away. Cook for 3 to 4 minutes and turn the salmon over. Cook until the interior of the salmon offers just a little bit of resistance when you squeeze its sides.

3. Remove the salmon from heat, sprinkle the lemon zest over it, and serve with lemon wedges.

WHOLE BRANZINO

1 to 2 lb. whole branzino

4 fresh basil leaves

1 tablespoon kosher salt

1 tablespoon black pepper

½ lemon

1. Prepare a fire, either setting up an even coal bed if you are able to adjust the height of your grate easily, or banking the coals to set up one zone for direct heat and another for indirect. Set up a grate over the coals.

2. Clean the branzino, remove the bones, and descale it. Pat it dry with paper towels and rub the flesh with the basil leaves. Season with the salt and pepper and close the fish back up.

3. Place your hand over the grate to test the heat in each section. Place the fish over medium-high heat—a spot you can leave your hand over for 3 or 4 seconds before you need to move it away. Cook until the fish is just cooked through and the skin is crispy, 10 to 12 minutes, turning the fish over just once.

4. Remove the fish from heat and place it on a large platter. Squeeze the lemon over it and enjoy.

WHOLE BRANZINO

See page 107

Yield: 6 Servings

Total Time: 1 Hour

MUSSELS IN WHITE WINE & HERBS

2 cups dry white wine

2 garlic cloves, minced

2 shallots, finely diced

¼ cup chopped fresh parsley

1 teaspoon fresh thyme

6 lbs. mussels, rinsed well and debearded

Salt, to taste

Crusty bread, for serving

1. Prepare a fire, either setting up an even coal bed if you are able to adjust the height of your grate easily, or banking the coals to set up one zone for direct heat and another for indirect. Set up a grate over the coals.

2. Place the wine, garlic, shallots, parsley, and thyme in a stockpot. Place your hand over the grate to test the heat in each section. Place the pot over medium heat—a spot you can leave your hand over for 5 seconds before you need to move it away—and bring the mixture to a simmer.

3. Add the mussels, partially cover the pot, and simmer for 3 to 4 minutes.

4. Stir to coat the mussels with the broth, partially cover the pot again, and cook until the majority of the mussels have opened, about 4 minutes. Discard any mussels that did not open.

5. Divide the mussels among the serving bowls. Strain the broth and season it with salt. Ladle the broth over the mussels and serve with crusty bread.

Yield: 6 Servings

Total Time: 1 Hour

ROMESCO DE PEIX

½ cup slivered almonds

½ teaspoon saffron

½ cup extra-virgin olive oil

1 large yellow onion, chopped

2 large red bell peppers, stems and seeds removed, chopped

2½ teaspoons sweet paprika

1 tablespoon smoked paprika

1 bay leaf

2 tablespoons tomato paste

½ cup sherry

2 cups Fish Stock (see page 246)

1 (28 oz.) can of diced tomatoes, with their liquid

Salt and pepper, to taste

1½ lbs. monkfish fillets, chopped into large pieces

1 lb. mussels, rinsed well and debearded

Fresh cilantro, finely chopped, for garnish

1. Place the almonds in a large cast-iron skillet and, on the stovetop, toast them over medium heat until they are just browned. Transfer them to a food processor and pulse until they are finely ground.

2. Place the saffron and ¼ cup boiling water in a bowl and let the saffron steep for 10 minutes.

3. Prepare a fire, either setting up an even coal bed if you are able to adjust the height of your grate easily, or banking the coals to set up one zone for direct heat and another for indirect. Set up a grate over the coals.

4. Place your hand over the grate to test the heat in each section. Place a Dutch oven over medium heat—a spot you can leave your hand over for 5 seconds before you need to move it away. Add the olive oil and warm it. Add the onion and bell peppers and cook, stirring occasionally, until the peppers are tender, about 10 minutes.

5. Add the sweet paprika, smoked paprika, bay leaf, and tomato paste and cook, stirring constantly, for 1 minute. Add the sherry and bring the mixture to a boil. Boil for 5 minutes and then stir in the stock, tomatoes, saffron, and the soaking liquid. Stir to combine, season with salt and pepper, and reduce the heat so that the soup simmers.

6. Stir in the ground almonds and cook until the mixture thickens slightly, about 8 minutes. Add the fish and mussels, stir gently to incorporate, and simmer until the fish is cooked through and a majority of the mussels have opened, about 5 minutes. Discard any mussels that do not open.

7. Ladle the mixture into warmed bowls, garnish with cilantro, and enjoy.

1¼ lb. lobster

1 lb. P.E.I. mussels, rinsed well and debearded

12 Littleneck clams, rinsed well and scrubbed

2 tablespoons extra-virgin olive oil

½ large fennel bulb, trimmed and sliced thin

2 shallots, minced

3 garlic cloves, minced

1 (6 oz.) can of tomato paste

1 cup red wine

1 (28 oz.) can of whole san marzano tomatoes, with their liquid, lightly crushed by hand

1 cup white wine

2 cups Fish Stock (see page 246)

2 bay leaves

1 teaspoon red pepper flakes

Salt and pepper, to taste

1 lb. halibut fillets, skin removed, cubed

Crusty bread, for serving

Yield: 6 Servings

Total Time: 1 Hour and 30 Minutes

LOBSTER CIOPPINO

1. Prepare a fire, either setting up an even coal bed if you are able to adjust the height of your grate easily, or banking the coals to set up one zone for direct heat and another for indirect. Set up a grate over the coals.

2. Place 3 inches of water in a Dutch oven. Place your hand over the grate to test the heat in each section. Place the Dutch oven over medium-high heat—a spot you can leave your hand over for 3 or 4 seconds before you need to move it away—and bring the water to a boil. Place the lobster, headfirst, in the pot, cover the pot, and cook the lobster until the shell is bright red, about 6 minutes. Remove the lobster from the pot and set it aside. Discard the cooking liquid and place the Dutch oven back over medium-high heat.

3. Add 2 cups of water to the pot and bring it to a boil. Add the mussels and clams, cover the pot, and cook until the majority of the mussels and clams have opened, about 5 minutes. Drain the mussels and clams, reserve the liquid, and set the mussels and clams aside. Discard any mussels and/or clams and that did not open.

4. Place the Dutch oven over medium-high heat and add the olive oil. Add the fennel and cook, stirring occasionally, until it has softened, about 5 minutes. Add the shallots and cook, stirring occasionally, until they have softened, about 5 minutes.

5. Add the garlic and tomato paste and cook, stirring continually, for 1 minute. Deglaze the pot with the red wine, scraping up any browned bits from the bottom of the pot. Cook until the wine has almost evaporated, about 5 minutes.

6. Add the tomatoes, white wine, stock, bay leaves, red pepper flakes, and a pinch of salt and pepper. Place the pot over medium-low heat—a spot you can leave your hand over for 6 or 7 seconds before you need to move it away—partially cover the pot, and cook the stew for 30 minutes.

7. While the stew is cooking, remove the meat from the tail and claws of the lobster. Set it aside.

8. Remove the legs from the lobster and add the remaining carcass to the pot. Uncover the pot and cook the stew for 20 minutes.

9. Add the halibut to the pot and cook until it is cooked through, about 5 minutes. Add the lobster meat, clams, mussels, and the reserved cooking liquid and cook until everything is warmed through, about 2 minutes.

10. Ladle the stew into warmed bowls and serve with crusty bread.

Yield: 6 Servings

Total Time: 1 Hour and 15 Minutes

JAMBALAYA

½ lb. andouille sausage

½ lb. shrimp, shells removed, deveined

¼ cup extra-virgin olive oil

4 boneless, skinless chicken thighs, chopped

2 yellow onions, chopped

1 large green bell pepper, stem and seeds removed, chopped

2 celery stalks, chopped

3 garlic cloves, minced

3 plum tomatoes, chopped

2 bay leaves

2 tablespoons paprika

2 tablespoons dried thyme

1 tablespoon garlic powder

1 tablespoon onion powder

1 teaspoon cayenne pepper

Salt and pepper, to taste

1½ cups long-grain white rice

2 tablespoons Worcestershire sauce

Hot sauce, to taste

3 cups Chicken Stock (see page 245)

Scallions, trimmed and chopped, for garnish

1. Prepare a fire, either setting up an even coal bed if you are able to adjust the height of your grate easily, or banking the coals to set up one zone for direct heat and another for indirect. Set up a grate over the coals.

2. Place your hand over the grate to test the heat in each section. Place the sausage and shrimp over medium-high heat—a spot you can leave your hand over for 3 or 4 seconds before you need to move it away. Cook the shrimp for 1 minute on each side, remove it from heat, and set it aside. Cook the sausage until it is browned all over, about 8 minutes. Remove the sausage from heat and set it aside.

3. Place the olive oil in a Dutch oven and place it over medium heat— a spot you can leave your hand over for 5 seconds before you need to move it away. Add the chicken, onions, bell pepper, and celery to the Dutch oven and cook, stirring occasionally, until the vegetables start to caramelize and the chicken is browned and cooked through, 6 to 8 minutes. Add the garlic and cook, stirring continually, for 1 minute.

4. Add the tomatoes, bay leaves, and all of the seasonings and simmer for 30 minutes, stirring occasionally.

5. Stir in the rice, Worcestershire sauce, hot sauce, and stock. Slice the sausage, return it to the pot, and place the Dutch oven over medium-low heat— a spot you can leave your hand over for 6 or 7 seconds before you need to move it away. Cover the Dutch oven and cook the jambalaya until the rice is tender, about 25 minutes.

6. Return the shrimp to the pot, cover it, and remove it from heat. Let the jambalaya sit for 5 minutes before ladling it into warmed bowls and garnishing with scallions.

Yield: 8 Servings

Total Time: 1 Hour and 15 Minutes

SHRIMP BOIL

¼ cup pickling spices

¼ cup kosher salt, plus more to taste

2 tablespoons mustard seeds

2 tablespoons black peppercorns

2 tablespoons red pepper flakes

1 tablespoon celery seeds

2 tablespoons ground ginger

2 teaspoons dried oregano

1 head of garlic, split in half horizontally

2 lbs. andouille sausage

2 lbs. russet potatoes

2 lbs. shrimp, shells removed, deveined

2 lemons, 1 juiced; 1 halved

¼ cup extra-virgin olive oil

Fresh parsley, chopped, for garnish

Remoulade Sauce
(see page 218), for serving

1. Prepare a fire, either setting up an even coal bed if you are able to adjust the height of your grate easily, or banking the coals to set up one zone for direct heat and another for indirect. Set up a grate over the coals.

2. Place the pickling spices, salt, mustard seeds, peppercorns, red pepper flakes, celery seeds, ginger, and oregano in a bowl and stir to combine. Set the seasoning mixture aside.

3. Place 12 cups water in a stockpot. Place your hand over the grate to test the heat in each section. Place the pot over high heat—a spot you can only leave your hand over for 2 seconds before you need to move it away—and bring the water to a boil.

4. Whisk in the seasoning mixture and bring the water back to a rapid simmer. Add the garlic, sausage, and potatoes, return to a simmer, and cover the pot with a lid. Cook until the potatoes are just tender, 10 to 15 minutes.

5. Remove the potatoes and sausage from the pot, place them on a platter, and set them aside. Stir the shrimp and lemon juice into the pot, partially cover the pot, and simmer the shrimp until they are pink and tender, about 5 minutes.

6. While the shrimp are cooking, cut the potatoes into wedges and the sausages in half. Place them in a large mixing bowl, drizzle the olive oil over them, and season with salt. Toss to combine.

7. Place the potatoes and sausages over medium heat—a spot you can leave your hand over for 5 seconds before you need to move it away—and cook until the potatoes are golden brown and the sausages are lightly charred, 5 to 8 minutes, turning them as necessary.

8. Drain the shrimp and arrange them on a platter along with the potatoes, sausage, and lemon halves. Garnish with parsley and serve with the Remoulade Sauce.

CAJUN TILAPIA

1½ lbs. tilapia fillets, each about ¾ inch thick

½ cup unsalted butter, melted

Cajun Rub (see page 208)

Lemon wedges, for serving

1. Prepare a fire, either setting up an even coal bed if you are able to adjust the height of your grate easily, or banking the coals to set up one zone for direct heat and another for indirect. Set up a grate over the coals.

2. Dip the tilapia in the melted butter and then apply the rub until the tilapia is generously coated on both sides.

3. Place your hand over the grate to test the heat in each section. Place the tilapia over high heat—a spot you can only leave your hand over for 2 seconds before you need to move it away. Cook until the tilapia is cooked through and lightly charred, about 6 minutes, turning it over just once. To determine if the inside is cooked enough, squeeze the sides of the tilapia. If the inside offers just a bit of resistance, it is ready.

4. Remove the tilapia from heat, serve with lemon wedges, and enjoy.

Yield: 4 Servings

Total Time: 1 Hour

HONEY & SOY-GLAZED RAINBOW TROUT

2 tablespoons honey

¼ cup soy sauce

2 large rainbow trout fillets, skin removed

Salt and pepper, to taste

1 lime, halved

Sesame seeds, for garnish

1. Prepare a fire, either setting up an even coal bed if you are able to adjust the height of your grate easily, or banking the coals to set up one zone for direct heat and another for indirect. Set up a grate over the coals.

2. Place the honey and soy sauce in a small bowl and stir until the honey has liquefied. Divide the glaze into two portions.

3. Place the trout on a plate, season it with salt and pepper, and brush it with half of the glaze. Place your hand over the grate to test the heat in each section. Place the trout over medium-high heat—a spot you can leave your hand over for 3 or 4 seconds before you need to move it away. Cook until the trout is cooked through and the exterior is lightly charred, about 6 minutes, turning it over just once. To determine if the inside is cooked enough, squeeze the sides of the trout. If the inside offers just a bit of resistance, it is ready.

4. Remove the trout from heat and place it on a platter. Spoon the remaining glaze over the trout and squeeze the lime over the top. Garnish the dish with sesame seeds and enjoy.

HONEY & SOY-GLAZED RAINBOW TROUT

See page 121

Yield: 4 Servings

Total Time: 1 Hour

LOBSTER MOJO DE AJO

10 oz. garlic cloves, unpeeled

1 cup plus 2 tablespoons unsalted butter

2 tablespoons guajillo chile powder

2 tablespoons chopped fresh cilantro

Salt, to taste

4 fresh lobster tails, split in half lengthwise so that the flesh is exposed

Lime wedges, for serving

1. Place the garlic in a dry skillet and, on the stovetop, toast it over medium heat until it is lightly charred in spots, about 10 minutes, turning occasionally. Remove the garlic from the pan and peel it.

2. Place the butter in a skillet and melt it over medium heat. Add the garlic and continue cooking until the butter begins to foam and brown slightly. Remove the pan from heat and let the mixture cool to room temperature.

3. Place the butter, garlic, guajillo powder, and cilantro in a blender and puree until smooth. Transfer three-quarters of the mojo de ajo to a large mixing bowl. Place the remaining mojo de ajo in a small bowl and set it aside. Let it cool completely.

4. Add the lobster tails to the mojo in the large mixing bowl and let them marinate for 30 minutes.

5. Prepare a fire, either setting up an even coal bed if you are able to adjust the height of your grate easily, or banking the coals to set up one zone for direct heat and another for indirect. Set up a grate over the coals.

6. Place the small bowl containing the reserved mojo de ajo beside the fire. Place your hand over the grate to test the heat in each section. Place the lobster tails, flesh side down, over high heat—a spot you can only leave your hand over for 2 seconds before you need to move it away. Cook until the flesh is caramelized and almost cooked through, 3 to 4 minutes.

7. Turn the lobster tails over and brush them with some of the reserved mojo de ajo. Cook until completely cooked through, 1 to 2 minutes.

8. Remove the lobster tails from heat and serve with lime wedges and any of the remaining reserved mojo de ajo.

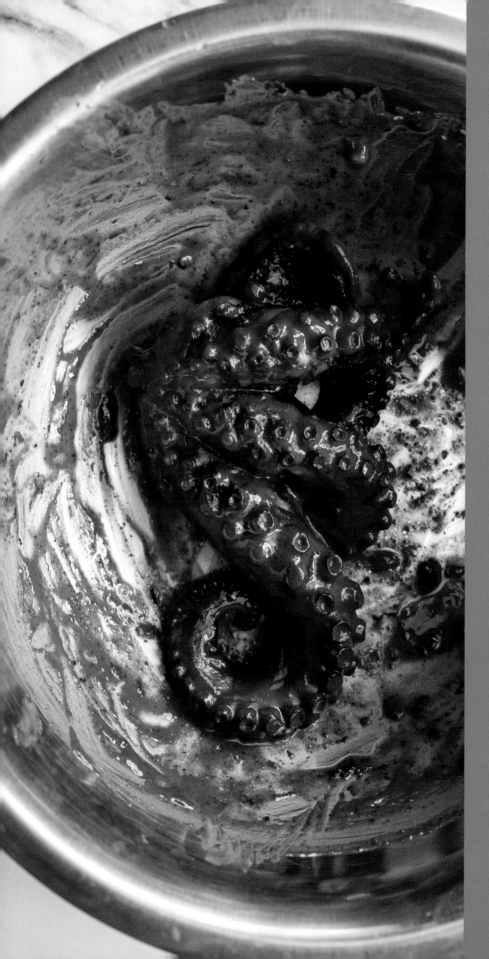

1 head of garlic, halved

1 white onion, quartered

3 allspice berries

2 whole cloves

½ cinnamon stick

3 chipotle morita chile peppers

2 dried chiles de àrbol

7 guajillo chile peppers

2 tablespoons fresh lime juice

2 tablespoons orange juice

2 tablespoons grapefruit juice

7 tablespoons pineapple juice

½ cup Recado Rojo (see page 215)

5 garlic cloves

⅛ teaspoon dried oregano

Salt, to taste

6 lb. octopus, beak removed and head cleaned

1 small bunch of fresh epazote

3 bay leaves

8 cups Chicken Stock (see page 245)

Corn Tortillas (see page 180), for serving

Lime wedges, for serving

Yield: 4 to 6 Servings

Total Time: 3 Hours

OCTOPUS AL PASTOR

1. Place the garlic and onion in a dry skillet and, on the stovetop, cook them over medium heat until they are lightly charred. Remove them from the pan and set them aside.

2. Add the allspice, cloves, and cinnamon stick to the skillet and toast until fragrant, shaking the pan frequently. Grind the spices into a powder using a mortar and pestle or a spice grinder.

3. Place the chiles in the skillet and toast over medium heat until they darken and become fragrant and pliable. Submerge them in a bowl of hot water and let them soak for 30 minutes.

4. Drain the chiles and reserve the liquid. Add the chiles, toasted spice powder, juices, Recado Rojo, garlic cloves (not the charred head of garlic), and oregano to a blender and puree until smooth, adding the reserved liquid as necessary to get the desired texture. Season the al pastor marinade with salt and set it aside.

5. Bring water to a boil in a large saucepan. Place the octopus in the boiling water and poach it for 3 minutes. Remove the octopus from the water and let it cool.

6. Prepare a fire, piling the coals in a large mound.

7. Place the octopus, epazote, bay leaves, head of garlic, and onion in a Dutch oven and add stock until half of the octopus is submerged. Cover the Dutch oven and carefully nestle it into the coals. Braise the octopus for 2 to 3 hours, until the thickest parts of the tentacles are very tender. Remove the octopus from the braising liquid and let it cool.

8. Place the octopus in the al pastor marinade and marinate it for 30 minutes. Even out the coal bed and set up a grate over it.

9. Remove the octopus from the marinade and shake to remove any excess. Place your hand over the grate to test the heat in each section. Place the octopus over high heat—a spot you can only leave your hand over for 2 seconds before you need to move it away. Cook until it is caramelized and crispy all over, about 5 to 7 minutes.

10. Remove the octopus from heat and serve it with tortillas and lime wedges.

Yield: 4 Servings

Total Time: 1 Hour and 15 Minutes

BBQ SHRIMP, NEW ORLEANS STYLE

2 lbs. jumbo shrimp, shells removed, deveined

1 teaspoon cayenne pepper

1 teaspoon dried thyme

1 teaspoon dried oregano

1 teaspoon sweet paprika

1 teaspoon dried rosemary

1 teaspoon garlic powder

2 tablespoons chopped fresh parsley, plus more for garnish

1 teaspoon kosher salt

1 teaspoon black pepper

2 tablespoons extra-virgin olive oil

Lemon wedges, for serving

1. Pat the shrimp dry with paper towels and place them in a large mixing bowl. Set the shrimp aside.

2. Place the cayenne, thyme, oregano, paprika, rosemary, garlic powder, parsley, salt, and pepper in a mixing bowl and stir until well combined. Sprinkle the mixture over the shrimp and toss to coat.

3. Drizzle the olive oil over the shrimp and toss to coat. Cover the bowl with plastic wrap and let the shrimp marinate in the refrigerator for 40 minutes.

4. Prepare a fire, either setting up an even coal bed if you are able to adjust the height of your grate easily, or banking the coals to set up one zone for direct heat and another for indirect. Set up a grate over the coals. If using bamboo skewers, soak them in water.

5. Thread the shrimp onto skewers. Place your hand over the grate to test the heat in each section. Place the skewers over high heat—a spot you can only leave your hand over for 2 seconds before you need to move it away. Cook until the shrimp turn pink and are cooked through, 3 to 5 minutes, turning them as necessary.

6. Remove the skewers from heat and garnish them with additional parsley. Serve with lemon wedges and enjoy.

Yield: 6 Servings

Total Time: 3 Hours

CEDAR-PLANK SALMON

2 tablespoons whole-grain mustard

2 tablespoons mild honey or pure maple syrup

1 teaspoon finely chopped fresh rosemary

1 tablespoon lemon zest

½ teaspoon kosher salt

½ teaspoon black pepper

2 lb. skin-on salmon fillet (about 1½ inches thick)

1. Soak a cedar grilling plank in water for 2 hours.

2. Prepare a fire, either setting up an even coal bed if you are able to adjust the height of your grate easily, or banking the coals to set up one zone for direct heat and another for indirect. Set up a grate over the coals.

3. Place the mustard, honey, rosemary, lemon zest, salt, and pepper in a bowl and stir until well combined. Spread the mixture over the salmon and let it stand at room temperature for 15 minutes.

4. Place the salmon on the plank, skin side down. Place your hand over the grate to test the heat in each section. Place the plank over medium-high heat—a spot you can leave your hand over for 3 or 4 seconds before you need to move it away. Cook until the salmon is just cooked through and the edges are browned, 13 to 15 minutes.

5. Remove the salmon from the grill and let it rest on the plank for 3 minutes before serving.

CEDAR-PLANK SALMON

Yield: 4 Servings

Total Time: 1 Hour

SALMON & VEGETABLE SKEWERS

3½ tablespoons fresh lime juice

2 garlic cloves, minced

1 bunch of fresh parsley, chopped

2 tablespoons extra-virgin olive oil

Salt and pepper, to taste

1 lb. salmon fillets, skin removed, cut into large cubes

2 celery stalks, cut into 1-inch pieces

1 yellow bell pepper, stem and seeds removed and cut into 1-inch pieces

16 cherry tomatoes

Lime wedges, for serving

1. Place the lime juice, garlic, parsley, olive oil, salt, and pepper in a large bowl and stir until well combined. Add the salmon, celery, bell pepper, and tomatoes and toss until well coated. Cover the bowl with plastic wrap and let the mixture marinate in the refrigerator for 30 minutes.

2. Prepare a fire, either setting up an even coal bed if you are able to adjust the height of your grate easily, or banking the coals to set up one zone for direct heat and another for indirect. Set up a grate over the coals. If using bamboo skewers, soak them in water.

3. Thread the salmon, celery, peppers, and tomatoes onto skewers, alternating between them.

4. Place your hand over the grate to test the heat in each section. Place the skewers over medium-high heat—a spot you can leave your hand over for 3 or 4 seconds before you need to move it away. Cook until the salmon is cooked through and the vegetables are tender, 8 to 10 minutes, turning the skewers as little as possible.

5. Remove the skewers from heat, serve with lime wedges, and enjoy.

TUNA WITH ORANGE & FENNEL SALAD

FOR THE TUNA

3½ tablespoons orange juice

3½ tablespoons soy sauce

1 tablespoon fresh lemon juice

2 tablespoons extra-virgin olive oil

2 tablespoons chopped fresh parsley

1 garlic clove, minced

½ teaspoon chopped fresh oregano

½ teaspoon black pepper

1 lb. tuna steaks

FOR THE SALAD

4 oranges

2 small fennel bulbs, trimmed and sliced thin

½ red onion, sliced thin

1 cup mesclun greens

2 tablespoons fresh lemon juice

1 tablespoon soy sauce

3½ tablespoons extra-virgin olive oil

Salt and pepper, to taste

1. To begin preparations for the tuna, place the orange juice, soy sauce, lemon juice, olive oil, parsley, garlic, oregano, and pepper in a baking dish. Place the tuna steaks in the marinade and turn until they are coated. Cover the dish with plastic wrap and marinate the tuna in the refrigerator for 1 hour.

2. To prepare the salad, peel the oranges and remove all of the white pith. Segment the oranges and reserve any juice. Place the orange segments, fennel, onion, and greens in a large bowl and toss to combine. Place the lemon juice, soy sauce, reserved orange juice, and olive oil in a small bowl, season the mixture with salt and pepper, and whisk until the dressing has emulsified. Drizzle the dressing over the salad and toss to coat. Set the salad aside.

3. Prepare a fire, either setting up an even coal bed if you are able to adjust the height of your grate easily, or banking the coals to set up one zone for direct heat and another for indirect. Set up a grate over the coals.

4. Place your hand over the grate to test the heat in each section. Place the tuna over high heat—a spot you can only leave your hand over for 2 seconds before you need to move it away. Grill until both sides of the tuna are seared and the interior is rare, about 1 minute per side.

5. Remove the tuna from heat and serve it alongside the salad.

TUNA WITH ORANGE & FENNEL SALAD

See page 133

Yield: 8 Servings

Total Time: 1 Hour and 20 Minutes

MANHATTAN CLAM CHOWDER

4 thick-cut slices of bacon

1 onion, finely diced

3 celery stalks, diced

1 green bell pepper, stems and seeds removed, diced

2 garlic cloves, minced

1 cup fresh clam juice

1 cup canned diced tomatoes, with their juices

20 clams

1 teaspoon fresh thyme

1 tablespoon chopped fresh parsley

Salt and pepper, to taste

1. Prepare a fire, either setting up an even coal bed if you are able to adjust the height of your grate easily, or banking the coals to set up one zone for direct heat and another for indirect. Set up a grate over the coals.

2. Place your hand over the grate to test the heat in each section. Place a Dutch oven over medium heat—a spot you can leave your hand over for 5 seconds before you need to move it away—and let it warm up for 2 minutes.

3. Place the bacon in the Dutch oven, cover it, and cook until the bacon is crispy, about 4 minutes. Transfer the bacon to a paper towel–lined plate and set it aside.

4. Add the onion, celery, and bell pepper to the Dutch oven and cook, stirring occasionally, until the vegetables are tender, about 8 minutes. Stir in the garlic and cook, stirring continually, for 1 minute.

5. Add the clam juice and tomatoes and cook for about 15 minutes, stirring occasionally.

6. Stir in the clams, thyme, and parsley and cover the Dutch oven. Cook until the majority of the clams have opened, about 6 to 8 minutes. Discard any clams that did not open.

7. Remove the Dutch oven from heat and season the chowder with salt and pepper. Ladle the chowder into warmed bowls and enjoy.

Yield: 6 Servings

Total Time: 1 Hour

CHERMOULA SEA BASS

6 sea bass fillets, skin removed, each about ¾ inch thick

3 tablespoons Chermoula Sauce (see page 219)

Lemon wedges, for serving

1. Rub the sea bass with the Chermoula Sauce. Place the sea bass in a baking dish and let it marinate in the refrigerator for 30 minutes.

2. Prepare a fire, either setting up an even coal bed if you are able to adjust the height of your grate easily, or banking the coals to set up one zone for direct heat and another for indirect. Set up a grate over the coals.

3. Place your hand over the grate to test the heat in each section. Place the sea bass over high heat—a spot you can only leave your hand over for 2 seconds before you need to move it away. Cook until the sea bass is just cooked through and lightly charred, about 6 minutes, turning it over just once. To determine if the inside is cooked enough, squeeze the sides of the sea bass. If the inside offers just a bit of resistance, it is ready.

4. Remove the sea bass from heat, let it rest for 2 minutes, and serve with lemon wedges.

Yield: 4 Servings

Total Time: 1 Hour

SWORDFISH

4 swordfish steaks, each about ¾ to 1 inch thick

1½ tablespoons extra-virgin olive oil

Seafood Rub (see page 199), to taste

Lemon wedges, for serving

1. Prepare a fire, either setting up an even coal bed if you are able to adjust the height of your grate easily, or banking the coals to set up one zone for direct heat and another for indirect. Set up a grate over the coals.

2. Rub the swordfish with the olive oil and then apply the rub until it is generously coated on both sides and let it rest at room temperature for 20 minutes.

3. Place your hand over the grate to test the heat in each section. Place the swordfish over medium-high heat—a spot you can leave your hand over for 3 or 4 seconds before you need to move it away. Cook until the swordfish is just cooked through and the exterior is nicely seared, about 6 minutes, turning it over just once. To determine if the inside is cooked enough, squeeze the sides of the swordfish. If the inside offers just a bit of resistance, it is ready.

4. Remove the swordfish from heat, let it rest for 2 minutes, and serve with lemon wedges.

SWORDFISH
See page 139

APPETIZERS,
SIDES & SALADS

Whether it be a light appetizer to invigorate the palate, a wholesome salad to temper a heavy entree, or a side that features the fruits of your labors in the garden, these recipes are sure to round out your table.

CANTALOUPE & MOZZARELLA WITH BALSAMIC GLAZE

1 cantaloupe

1 tablespoon extra-virgin olive oil

4 oz. fresh mozzarella cheese, torn

1 tablespoon Balsamic Glaze (see page 242)

Fresh parsley, chopped, for garnish

1. Remove the rind from the cantaloupe, halve it, remove the seeds, and then cut the cantaloupe into ½-inch-thick slices. Set the cantaloupe aside.

2. Prepare a fire, either setting up an even coal bed if you are able to adjust the height of your grate easily, or banking the coals to set up one zone for direct heat and another for indirect. Set up a grate over the coals.

3. Place the cantaloupe in a mixing bowl, add the olive oil, and toss to coat.

4. Place your hand over the grate to test the heat in each section. Place the cantaloupe over medium-high heat—a spot you can leave your hand over for 3 or 4 seconds before you need to move it away. Grill until the cantaloupe is lightly charred on both sides and warmed through, 4 to 6 minutes.

5. To serve, pile the warm cantaloupe on a plate, top with the mozzarella, and drizzle the Balsamic Glaze over the top. Garnish with parsley and enjoy.

Yield: 2 Servings

Total Time: 1 Hour

FIG & GOAT CHEESE SALAD

1 cup Pinot Noir

¼ cup sugar

4 orange slices

6 fresh figs, halved

2 tablespoons crumbled goat cheese

1. Place the wine and sugar in a small saucepan and warm the mixture over medium-high heat, stirring until the sugar has dissolved. Simmer until the mixture has reduced to a syrupy consistency. Remove the pan from heat and set it aside.

2. Prepare a fire, either setting up an even coal bed if you are able to adjust the height of your grate easily, or banking the coals to set up one zone for direct heat and another for indirect. Set up a grate over the coals.

3. Place your hand over the grate to test the heat in each section. Place the orange slices over medium-high heat—a spot you can leave your hand over for 3 or 4 seconds before you need to move it away. Cook until the orange slices are caramelized on each side, about 2 minutes. Remove them from the grill and set them aside.

4. Place the figs on the grill, cut side down, and cook until they are lightly browned and soft, about 4 minutes.

5. To serve, place the orange slices on a plate, place the figs on top of the orange slices, and sprinkle the goat cheese over the dish. Drizzle the reduction over the top and enjoy.

Yield: 4 Servings

Total Time: 1 Hour and 30 Minutes

VEGETABLE KEBABS

¼ cup extra-virgin olive oil

2 teaspoons Dijon mustard

2 garlic cloves, minced

2 teaspoons red wine vinegar

2 teaspoons honey

1 teaspoon chopped fresh rosemary

Salt and pepper, to taste

2 portobello mushrooms, stems removed, cut into 1-inch cubes

2 zucchini, cut into 1-inch cubes

1 red bell pepper, stem and seeds removed, cut into 1-inch squares

1 green bell pepper, stem and seeds removed, cut into 1-inch squares

1. If using bamboo skewers, soak them in water.

2. Place the olive oil, the mustard, garlic, vinegar, honey, and rosemary in a mixing bowl and whisk to combine. Season the dressing with salt and pepper and set it aside.

3. Thread the vegetables onto skewers and place them on a baking sheet. Pour the dressing over the skewers, cover them with plastic wrap, and let them marinate at room temperature for 1 hour, turning occasionally.

4. Prepare a fire, either setting up an even coal bed if you are able to adjust the height of your grate easily, or banking the coals to set up one zone for direct heat and another for indirect. Set up a grate over the coals.

5. Remove the vegetable skewers from the dressing and reserve the dressing. Place your hand over the grate to test the heat in each section. Place the kebabs over medium heat—a spot you can leave your hand over for 5 seconds before you need to move it away. Grill until the vegetables are tender and lightly charred, 10 to 12 minutes, turning them as little as possible.

6. Remove the skewers from heat and place them in a serving dish. Pour the reserved dressing over them and enjoy.

Yield: 4 Servings

Total Time: 10 Minutes

RAITA

1 cup full-fat yogurt

2 teaspoons minced red onion

½ cup deseeded and chopped Persian cucumber

2 tablespoons chopped fresh cilantro

1 teaspoon fresh lemon juice

I. Place all of the ingredients in a mixing bowl and stir to combine. Use immediately or cover the bowl and store in the refrigerator.

Yield: 4 Servings

Total Time: 2 Hours

GRILLED BEETS WITH DUKKAH

2 large beets

Pinch of kosher salt

2 tablespoons chopped walnuts

2 tablespoons chopped hazelnuts

2 tablespoons chopped pistachios

2 teaspoons black pepper

2 teaspoons poppy seeds

2 teaspoons black sesame seeds

Full-fat Greek yogurt, for serving

1 cinnamon stick

1. Place the beets and salt in a saucepan with at least 5 cups of water and bring to a boil. Cook the beets until a knife can easily pass through them, 30 to 40 minutes.

2. Drain the beets, run them under cold water, and peel off the skins and stems; it is easiest to do this while the beets are still hot.

3. Cut the peeled beets into ¾-inch cubes and set them aside.

4. Prepare a fire, either setting up an even coal bed if you are able to adjust the height of your grate easily, or banking the coals to set up one zone for direct heat and another for indirect. Set up a grate over the coals.

5. Place the nuts in a resealable bag and use a rolling pin to crush them. Transfer them to a small bowl, add the black pepper and seeds, and stir to combine. Set the dukkah aside.

6. Place your hand over the grate to test the heat in each section. Place the beets over high heat—a spot you can only leave your hand over for 2 seconds before you need to move it away. Cook until the beets are lightly charred all over, about 5 minutes, turning them as necessary.

7. Remove the beets from heat. To serve, spread the yogurt across a shallow bowl, pile the beets on top, and sprinkle the dukkah over the dish. Grate the cinnamon stick over the beets until the dish is to your taste and enjoy.

GRILLED BEETS
WITH DUKKAH

See page 149

Yield: 6 Servings

Total Time: 1 Hour and 15 Minutes

ELOTES

---

6 ears of corn, unshucked

3 chipotle chile peppers in adobo

½ cup mayonnaise

¼ cup sour cream

1½ tablespoons brown sugar

1 tablespoon fresh lime juice

2 tablespoons chopped cilantro, plus more for garnish

1 teaspoon kosher salt, plus more to taste

½ teaspoon black pepper, plus more to taste

3 tablespoons extra-virgin olive oil

½ cup crumbled goat cheese

Lime wedges, for serving

1. Prepare a fire, either setting up an even coal bed if you are able to adjust the height of your grate easily, or banking the coals to set up one zone for direct heat and another for indirect. Set up a grate over the coals.

2. Place your hand over the grate to test the heat in each section. Place the corn over medium-low heat—a spot you can leave your hand over for 6 or 7 seconds before you need to move it away. Cook until the kernels have a slight give to them, about 25 minutes.

3. Remove the corn from heat and let it cool. When the corn is cool enough to handle, shuck it.

4. Place the chipotles, mayonnaise, sour cream, brown sugar, lime juice, cilantro, salt, and pepper in a food processor and blitz until smooth. Set the mixture aside.

5. Drizzle the olive oil over the corn and season it with salt and pepper. Place the corn over medium-high heat—a spot you can leave your hand over for 3 or 4 seconds before you need to move it away. Cook until the corn is charred all over, about 5 minutes, turning it as necessary.

6. Remove the corn from heat and spread the mayonnaise mixture over it. Sprinkle the goat cheese over the top, garnish with additional cilantro, and serve with lime wedges.

Yield: 6 Servings
Total Time: 10 Minutes

MUSAENGCHAE

3 cups shredded daikon radish

1 teaspoon gochugaru

2 tablespoons rice vinegar

1 tablespoon kosher salt

1 tablespoon sugar

1. Place all of the ingredients in a bowl and stir to combine.

2. Let the musaengchae marinate in the refrigerator for 1 hour before serving.

Yield: 4 Servings

Total Time: 1 Hour

GRILLED OYSTERS

Handful of bay leaves

12 oysters, rinsed and scrubbed

7 tablespoons extra-virgin olive oil

7 tablespoons fresh lime juice

1 cup chopped fresh cilantro

1. Prepare a fire, either setting up an even coal bed if you are able to adjust the height of your grate easily, or banking the coals to set up one zone for direct heat and another for indirect. Set up a grate over the coals.

2. Distribute the bay leaves over the coals and set up a grate over them.

3. Place your hand over the grate to test the heat in each section. Place the oysters over medium-high heat—a spot you can leave your hand over for 3 or 4 seconds before you need to move it away. Cook until they start to open and absorb the smoke. Using tongs, carefully remove the oysters and arrange them on a platter or serving board.

4. Place the olive oil, lime juice, and cilantro in a bowl and stir until thoroughly combined. Serve this sauce alongside the oysters.

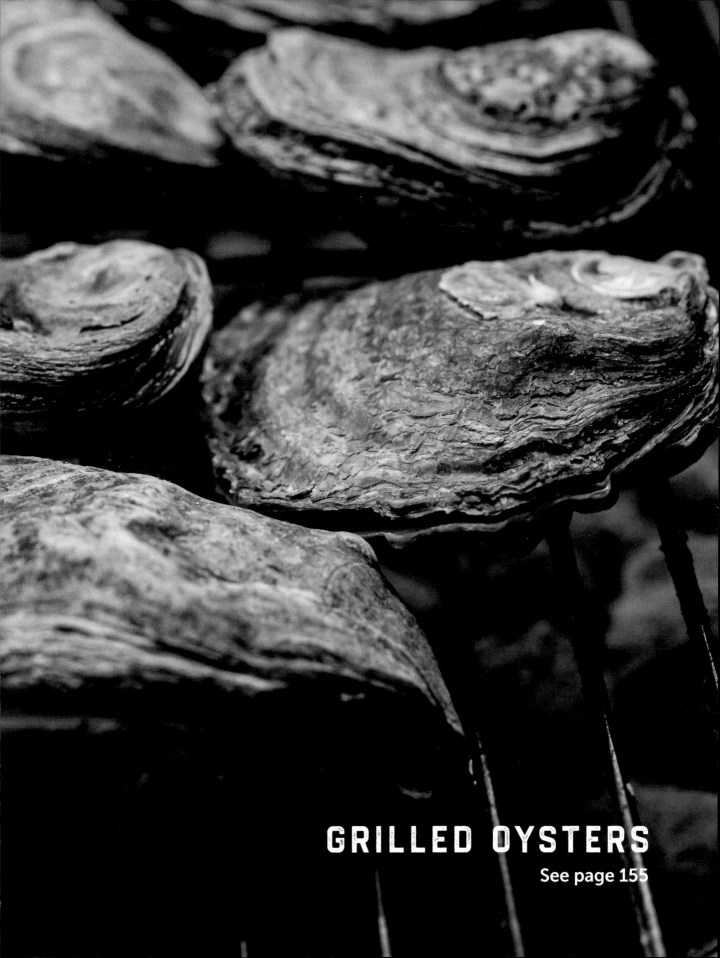

GRILLED OYSTERS
See page 155

Yield: 4 Servings

Total Time: 1 Hour

GRILLED CABBAGE

1 large head of green cabbage

2 tablespoons extra-virgin olive oil

1½ teaspoons garlic powder

Salt and pepper, to taste

1. Prepare a fire, either setting up an even coal bed if you are able to adjust the height of your grate easily, or banking the coals to set up one zone for direct heat and another for indirect. Set up a grate over the coals.

2. Cut the head of cabbage into 8 wedges. Remove the core, brush the wedges with olive oil, and season them with the garlic powder, salt, and pepper.

3. Place your hand over the grate to test the heat in each section. Place the cabbage over medium-high heat—a spot you can leave your hand over for 3 or 4 seconds before you need to move it away. Cook the cabbage until it is charred and tender, about 10 minutes, trying to turn it as little as possible.

4. Remove the cabbage from the grill and serve immediately.

Yield: 4 Servings

Total Time: 1 Hour

SUMMER SQUASH SALAD

1 tablespoon Dijon mustard

¼ cup plus 1 tablespoon extra-virgin olive oil

3 tablespoons balsamic vinegar

3 tablespoons red wine vinegar

1 lb. yellow squash, sliced lengthwise

1 large zucchini, sliced lengthwise

3 cups baby spinach

½ cup cherry tomatoes, halved

6 fresh basil leaves, chopped

3 fresh mint leaves, chopped

⅓ cup feta cheese, crumbled

1. Place the Dijon mustard, ¼ cup of olive oil, the balsamic vinegar, and red wine vinegar in a bowl and whisk until well combined. Set the dressing aside.

2. Place the squash and zucchini in a bowl, add the remaining olive oil, and toss to coat. Set the squash and zucchini aside.

3. Prepare a fire, either setting up an even coal bed if you are able to adjust the height of your grate easily, or banking the coals to set up one zone for direct heat and another for indirect. Set up a grate over the coals.

4. Place your hand over the grate to test the heat in each section. Place the squash and zucchini over medium-high heat—a spot you can leave your hand over for 3 or 4 seconds before you need to move it away. Cook until the vegetables are charred and tender, 6 to 8 minutes, turning them over just once.

5. Remove the squash and zucchini from heat and cut them into bite-size pieces. Place them in a salad bowl, add the spinach, cherry tomatoes, basil, mint, and dressing, and toss to coat.

6. Top the salad with the feta and enjoy.

Yield: 4 Servings

Total Time: 1 Hour

CHARRED EGGPLANT

1 onion, quartered

1 large eggplant, trimmed and halved lengthwise

1 red bell pepper

2 teaspoons kosher salt

¼ cup avocado oil

¼ cup balsamic vinegar

1. Prepare a fire, either setting up an even coal bed if you are able to adjust the height of your grate easily, or banking the coals to set up one zone for direct heat and another for indirect. Set up a grate over the coals.

2. Place your hand over the grate to test the heat in each section. Place the onion, eggplant, and pepper over medium heat—a spot you can leave your hand over for 5 seconds before you need to move it away. Cook until the onion and pepper are tender and lightly charred, and the eggplant has collapsed. This will take 15 to 20 minutes for the onion and pepper and 25 to 30 minutes for the eggplant.

3. Remove the vegetables from heat. Place the pepper in a bowl and cover it with aluminum foil. Let it steam for 5 minutes. Chop the eggplant and place it in a serving dish. Place the onion in a food processor and blitz until it is pureed. Spread the puree over a serving dish.

4. Remove the pepper from the bowl and chop it into bite-size pieces. Add it to the bowl containing the eggplant along with the salt, avocado oil, and balsamic vinegar. Toss to coat, pile the mixture on top of the onion puree, and enjoy.

CHARRED EGGPLANT

See page 161

Yield: 4 Servings

Total Time: 1 Hour

FIRE-ROASTED PEPPERS & ONIONS

2 bell peppers

2 red onions, halved

Salt, to taste

Extra-virgin olive oil, to taste

1. Prepare a fire, either setting up an even coal bed if you are able to adjust the height of your grate easily, or banking the coals to set up one zone for direct heat and another for indirect. Set up a grate over the coals.

2. Place your hand over the grate to test the heat in each section. Place the peppers and onions over low heat—a section of the grill you can comfortably leave your hand over for 9 seconds. Roast the vegetables until they are tender and charred all over, about 40 minutes for the onions and 25 minutes for the peppers. Turn the vegetables as little as necessary as they roast.

3. Transfer the peppers to a metal mixing bowl, cover the bowl with plastic wrap, and let them steam for 10 minutes. Place the onions on a cutting board and let them cool slightly.

4. Peel the peppers and remove the stems and seed pods. Chop them and place them in a bowl. When the onions are cool enough to handle, chop them and add them to the bowl.

5. Season the mixture with salt and drizzle a generous amount of olive oil over the top. Toss to combine and enjoy.

Yield: 4 Servings

Total Time: 1 Hour

GRILLED ASPARAGUS

1 bunch of asparagus, trimmed

3 tablespoons extra-virgin olive oil

½ teaspoon kosher salt

½ teaspoon black pepper

2 lemon wedges

1. Prepare a fire, either setting up an even coal bed if you are able to adjust the height of your grate easily, or banking the coals to set up one zone for direct heat and another for indirect. Set up a grate over the coals.

2. Place the asparagus in a baking dish, drizzle the olive oil over the top, and season it with the salt and pepper. Toss to coat.

3. Place your hand over the grate to test the heat in each section. Place the asparagus over medium heat—a spot you can leave your hand over for 5 seconds before you need to move it away. Cook until the asparagus is browned and tender, about 10 minutes, turning it as necessary.

4. Remove the asparagus from heat, squeeze the juice of the lemon wedges over it, and enjoy.

Yield: 4 Servings

Total Time: 1 Hour

GRILLED LEEKS WITH ROMESCO

4 leeks, trimmed, rinsed well, and halved lengthwise

2 tablespoons extra-virgin olive oil

Salt and pepper, to taste

Romesco Sauce (see page 236), for serving

1. Prepare a fire, either setting up an even coal bed if you are able to adjust the height of your grate easily, or banking the coals to set up one zone for direct heat and another for indirect. Set up a grate over the coals.

2. Place your hand over the grate to test the heat in each section. Place the leeks, cut side down, over medium-high heat—a spot you can leave your hand over for 3 or 4 seconds before you need to move it away. Cook until the leeks are charred on both sides and tender, 8 to 12 minutes, turning them over just once.

3. Remove the leeks from the grill, chop them, and place them in a serving dish. Drizzle the olive oil over the leeks, season them with salt and pepper, and serve alongside the Romesco Sauce.

Yield: 2 Servings

Total Time: 1 Hour

GRILLED ROMAINE & SWEET POTATO

Canola oil, as needed

1 cup shredded baked sweet potato skins

1 tablespoon kosher salt

2 teaspoons black pepper

½ green apple

½ cup white vinegar

1 heart of romaine lettuce

2 teaspoons extra-virgin olive oil

1 tablespoon balsamic vinegar

2 tablespoons crumbled feta cheese

I. Add canola oil to a small saucepan until it is about 2 inches deep and warm it to 350°F on the stovetop. Add the sweet potato skins and fry until golden brown and crispy, about 1 minute. Remove the fried sweet potato skins from the oil and place them on a paper towel–lined plate. Season the potato skins with 1 teaspoon of the salt and 1 teaspoon of the pepper.

2. Prepare a fire, either setting up an even coal bed if you are able to adjust the height of your grate easily, or banking the coals to set up one zone for direct heat and another for indirect. Set up a grate over the coals.

3. Cut the apple into ½-inch slices, leaving the skin on. Place the apple in a small bowl, add the white vinegar and 1 teaspoon of the salt, and toss to coat. Set the mixture aside.

4. Cut off the stem from the heart of romaine, separate the leaves, and place them in a bowl. Add the olive oil, remaining salt, and remaining pepper and toss to coat.

5. Place your hand over the grate to test the heat in each section. Place the romaine lettuce over high heat—a spot you can only leave your hand over for 2 seconds before you need to move it away. Cook the lettuce until it is slightly charred on both sides, but before it starts to wilt, about 1 minute.

6. Arrange the lettuce on a plate, crumble the fried sweet potato skins over them, and distribute the apple on top. Drizzle the balsamic over the dish, sprinkle the feta on top, and enjoy.

GRILLED ROMAINE & SWEET POTATO

See page 169

Yield: 6 Servings

Total Time: 24 Hours

SPICY TURKEY WINGS

4 lbs. turkey wings, separated into drumettes and flats

¼ cup hot sauce, plus more to taste

3 tablespoons extra-virgin olive oil

Salt, to taste

4 tablespoons unsalted butter, melted

1. Pat the wings dry with paper towels. Place the wings in a resealable plastic bag and add the hot sauce, olive oil, and salt. Toss to coat the wings and let them marinate in the refrigerator overnight.

2. Prepare a fire, either setting up an even coal bed if you are able to adjust the height of your grate easily, or banking the coals to set up one zone for direct heat and another for indirect. Set up a grate over the coals.

3. Place your hand over the grate to test the heat in each section. Place the wings over medium-low heat—a spot you can leave your hand over for 6 or 7 seconds before you need to move it away. Cook for 20 minutes.

4. Turn the wings over and cook until they are cooked through and crispy, about 8 minutes.

5. Remove the wings from the grill, place them in a bowl, and add the butter and additional hot sauce. Toss to coat and enjoy.

Yield: 8 Servings

Total Time: 1 Hour

CHORIZO-STUFFED MUSHROOMS

1 link of chorizo, casing removed

14 button mushrooms, stems removed

6 tablespoons extra-virgin olive oil

1 onion, finely diced

4 cherry tomatoes, minced

1 teaspoon fresh thyme

¼ cup Chicken Stock (see page 245)

1 small bunch of fresh parsley, chopped

¼ cup grated Parmesan cheese

Salt and pepper, to taste

1. Prepare a fire, either setting up an even coal bed if you are able to adjust the height of your grate easily, or banking the coals to set up one zone for direct heat and another for indirect. Set up a grate over the coals.

2. Place the chorizo in a food processor and blitz until it is a thick paste. Set the chorizo aside.

3. Brush the mushroom caps with 2 tablespoons of the olive oil. Place your hand over the grate to test the heat in each section. Place the mushroom caps over medium-high heat—a spot you can leave your hand over for 3 or 4 seconds before you need to move it away. Cook until the tops have browned, about 2 minutes. Remove the mushroom caps from the grill and set them aside.

4. Place the remaining olive oil in a cast-iron skillet and place it over medium-high heat. Add the onion, cherry tomatoes, and thyme and cook, stirring occasionally, until the onion is translucent, about 3 minutes.

5. Stir in the chorizo and cook until it is browned, about 7 minutes. Add the stock and parsley and cook for another minute. Remove the pan from heat.

6. Stuff the mushroom caps with the chorizo mixture and place them in a clean cast-iron skillet. Sprinkle some Parmesan over each stuffed mushroom and place the pan over medium-low heat—a spot you can leave your hand over for 6 or 7 seconds before you need to move it away. Cook until the mushrooms are cooked through, about 10 minutes.

7. Remove the pan from heat, season the stuffed mushrooms with salt and pepper, and enjoy.

Yield: 2 Servings

Total Time: 1 Hour

GRILLED GOAT CHEESE

½ lb. goat cheese, sliced into 10 rounds

10 tablespoons extra-virgin olive oil

1 teaspoon red wine vinegar

1 cup salt-cured black olives, pitted, patted dry, and chopped

¼ cup chopped walnuts

Red pepper flakes, to taste

2 teaspoons chopped fresh oregano

1 baguette, sliced

Salt and pepper, to taste

I. Place the goat cheese on a plate and chill it in the freezer.

2. Place ½ cup of olive oil, red wine vinegar, olives, walnuts, red pepper flakes, and oregano in a bowl and stir to combine. Set the mixture aside.

3. Prepare a fire, either setting up an even coal bed if you are able to adjust the height of your grate easily, or banking the coals to set up one zone for direct heat and another for indirect. Set up a grate over the coals.

4. Place your hand over the grate to test the heat in each section. Place a large cast-iron skillet over high heat—a spot you can leave your hand over for only 2 seconds before you need to move it away. Let the pan warm up for 10 minutes.

5. Brush both sides of the sliced baguette with some of the remaining olive oil. Place the baguette over medium-low heat—a spot you can leave your hand over for 6 or 7 seconds before you need to move it away. Toast the bread until lightly charred on both sides, 5 to 7 minutes. Remove the baguette slices from heat and set them aside.

6. Place the goat cheese in a single layer in the hot pan and cook until brown and crusty on the bottom, about 2 minutes. Carefully remove the goat cheese from the pan and arrange the rounds on the grilled slices of baguette. Spoon the olive mixture over the cheese, season with salt and pepper, and enjoy.

GRILLED SARDINES WITH LEMON & HERBS

Fresh sardines, scaled, gutted, and cleaned

Juice of 2 lemons

¼ cup extra-virgin olive oil

3 garlic cloves, minced

1 small shallot, minced

2 tablespoons chopped fresh parsley

1 tablespoon fresh cilantro

Salt and pepper, to taste

1. Arrange the sardines in a small baking dish. Drizzle the lemon juice and olive oil over them, place them in the refrigerator, and let them marinate for 30 minutes.

2. Prepare a fire, either setting up an even coal bed if you are able to adjust the height of your grate easily, or banking the coals to set up one zone for direct heat and another for indirect. Set up a grate over the coals. If using bamboo skewers, soak them in water.

3. Place the garlic, shallot, parsley, and cilantro in a small bowl and stir to combine. Stuff the sardines with the mixture, season them with salt and pepper, and thread them onto skewers.

4. Place your hand over the grate to test the heat in each section. Place the skewered sardines over medium heat—a spot you can leave your hand over for 5 seconds before you need to move it away. Cook until they are charred on both sides and their flesh is opaque, around 4 minutes, turning them over just once.

5. Remove the sardines from heat and let them rest for 2 minutes before enjoying.

NOTE: Sardines have a strong "fishiness" to them. As such, be sure to serve these with a glass of white wine to help mellow the taste buds before the main course.

GRILLED SARDINES
WITH LEMON & HERBS

See page 177

Yield: 32 Tortillas

Total Time: 30 Minutes

CORN TORTILLAS

1 lb. masa harina

1½ tablespoons kosher salt

3 cups warm filtered water, plus more as needed

1. In the work bowl of stand mixer fitted with the paddle attachment, combine the masa harina and salt. With the mixer on low speed, slowly begin to add the water. The mixture should come together as a soft, smooth dough. You want the masa to be moist enough so that when a small ball of it is pressed flat in your hands the edges do not crack. Also, the masa should not stick to your hands when you peel it off your palm.

2. Let the masa rest for 10 minutes and check the hydration again. You may need to add more water depending on environmental conditions.

3. On the stovetop, warm a cast-iron skillet over high heat. Portion the masa into 1-ounce balls and cover them with a damp linen towel.

4. Line a tortilla press with two 8-inch circles of plastic. You can use a grocery store bag, a resealable bag, or even a standard kitchen trash bag as a source for the plastic. Place a masa ball in the center of one circle and gently push down on it with the palm of one hand to flatten. Place the other plastic circle on top and then close the tortilla press, applying firm, even pressure to flatten the masa into a round tortilla.

5. Open the tortilla press and remove the top layer of plastic. Carefully pick up the tortilla and remove the bottom piece of plastic.

6. Gently lay the tortilla flat in the pan, taking care to not wrinkle it. Cook for 15 to 30 seconds, until the edge begins to lift up slightly. Turn the tortilla over and let it cook for 30 to 45 seconds before turning it over one last time. If the hydration of the masa was correct and the heat is high enough, the tortilla should puff up and inflate. Remove the tortilla from the pan and store it in a tortilla warmer lined with a linen towel. Repeat until all of the prepared masa has been made into tortillas.

SUCCOTASH

4 slices of thick-cut bacon

2 tablespoons unsalted butter

1 red onion, minced

4 cups canned corn

1 cup cherry tomatoes, halved

2 cups canned lima beans

Salt and pepper, to taste

1 tablespoon chopped fresh marjoram

¼ cup chopped fresh basil

1. On the stovetop, place a large cast-iron skillet over medium heat, add the bacon, and cook until crispy, about 8 minutes, turning it as necessary. Remove the bacon from the pan and place it on a paper towel–lined plate to drain. When it is cool enough to handle, crumble the bacon into bite-size pieces.

2. Place the butter in the skillet and melt it over medium-high heat. Add the onion and cook, stirring occasionally, until it is translucent, about 3 minutes.

3. Add the corn, cherry tomatoes, and lima beans and cook, stirring frequently, until the corn is tender, about 3 minutes.

4. Season the mixture with salt and pepper, stir in the marjoram, basil, and crumbled bacon, and enjoy.

Yield: 6 Servings
Total Time: 25 Minutes

COLESLAW

¼ cup apple cider vinegar

¼ cup honey

1 garlic clove, minced

1 teaspoon celery salt

1 teaspoon black pepper

1 teaspoon kosher salt

½ teaspoon mustard powder

½ head of red cabbage, core removed, shredded

½ head of green cabbage, core removed, shredded

2 carrots, peeled and shredded

1. Place all of the ingredients, except for the cabbages and carrots, in a saucepan on the stovetop and bring to a boil. Reduce the heat, simmer for 5 minutes, and remove the pan from heat.

2. Place the cabbages and carrots in a heatproof bowl, pour the dressing over it, and stir to combine.

3. Refrigerate the coleslaw for 30 minutes before serving.

SMOKY & SPICY CHICKEN WINGS

2 lbs. chicken wings, separated into drumettes and flats

2 tablespoons extra-virgin olive oil

Juice of ½ lime

3 garlic cloves, minced

2 tablespoons chopped fresh parsley

1 tablespoon cumin

2 teaspoons smoked paprika

1 teaspoon cinnamon

1 teaspoon turmeric

1 teaspoon red pepper flakes

½ teaspoon onion powder

Salt and pepper, to taste

1. Place the chicken wings on a baking sheet and put them in the refrigerator. Let them rest for at least 2 hours so that the skin on the wings tightens, which will promote crispy wings.

2. Place the wings in a large bowl, add the olive oil, and toss to coat. Place all of the remaining ingredients in another bowl, add the wings, and toss until they are evenly coated.

3. Prepare a fire, either setting up an even coal bed if you are able to adjust the height of your grate easily, or banking the coals to set up one zone for direct heat and another for indirect. Set up a grate over the coals.

4. Place your hand over the grate to test the heat in each section. Place the wings over medium-low heat—a spot you can leave your hand over for 6 or 7 seconds before you need to move it away. Cook for 20 minutes.

5. Turn the wings over and cook until they are cooked through and crispy, about 8 minutes.

6. Remove the wings from the grate and enjoy.

Yield: 4 Servings

Total Time: 3 Hours

BUFFALO WINGS

2 lbs. chicken wings, split

2 tablespoons Clarified Butter (see page 241)

3 garlic cloves, minced

¼ teaspoon cayenne pepper

¼ teaspoon paprika

2 teaspoons Tabasco

¼ cup Frank's hot sauce

Celery, cut into 3-inch pieces, for serving

1. Place the chicken wings on a roasting pan and place them in the refrigerator. Chill for at least 2 hours so that the skin on the chicken wings tightens, which will promote a crisper wing.

2. Place the Clarified Butter in a saucepan on the stovetop and warm it over medium heat. Add the garlic and cook, stirring continually, for 1 minute. Stir in the cayenne, paprika, Tabasco, and hot sauce and bring to a simmer over medium heat. Simmer for 3 minutes. Transfer the sauce to a mixing bowl and set it aside.

3. Prepare a fire, either setting up an even coal bed if you are able to adjust the height of your grate easily, or banking the coals to set up one zone for direct heat and another for indirect. Set up a grate over the coals.

4. Remove the chicken wings from the refrigerator, place them in the buffalo sauce, and toss to coat.

5. Place your hand over the grate to test the heat in each section. Place the chicken wings over medium-high heat—a spot you can leave your hand over for 3 or 4 seconds before you need to move it away. Cook the chicken wings until they are crispy and cooked through, 3 to 5 minutes per side.

6. Remove the wings from the grill, place them on a large serving platter, and serve alongside celery.

BUFFALO WINGS

Yield: 8 Servings

Total Time: 3 Hours

PITA BREAD

1 cup lukewarm water (90°F)

1 tablespoon active dry yeast

1 tablespoon sugar

1¾ cups all-purpose flour, plus more as needed

1 cup whole wheat flour

1 tablespoon kosher salt

1. In a large mixing bowl, combine the water, yeast, and sugar. Let the mixture sit until it starts to foam, about 15 minutes.

2. Add the flours and salt and work the mixture until it comes together as a smooth dough. Cover the bowl with a linen towel and let it rise for about 15 minutes.

3. Preheat the oven to 500°F and place a baking stone on the floor of the oven.

4. Divide the dough into eight pieces and form them into balls. Place the balls on a flour-dusted work surface, press them down, and roll them until they are about ¼ inch thick.

5. Working with one pita at a time, place the pita on the baking stone and bake until it is puffy and brown, about 8 minutes. Remove from the oven and serve warm or at room temperature.

CHICKEN TSUKUNE

2 lbs. chicken thighs, ground

1 large egg, lightly beaten

1 cup panko

2 teaspoons miso paste

2 tablespoons sake

1½ tablespoons mirin

½ teaspoon black pepper

Sesame seeds, for garnish

2 scallions, trimmed and sliced, for garnish

Tare Sauce (see page 231), for serving

1. Place the ground chicken, egg, bread crumbs, miso, sake, mirin, and the pepper in a bowl and stir to combine. Cover the bowl and place it in the refrigerator while you prepare a fire.

2. Prepare a fire, either setting up an even coal bed if you are able to adjust the height of your grate easily, or banking the coals to set up one zone for direct heat and another for indirect. Set up a grate over the coals.

3. Remove the chicken mixture from the refrigerator, form it into balls or ovals, and thread the meatballs onto skewers.

4. Place your hand over the grate to test the heat in each section. Place the meatballs over medium-high heat—a spot you can leave your hand over for 3 or 4 seconds before you need to move it away. Cook until they are browned all over and cooked through, 6 to 8 minutes, turning them as necessary.

5. Remove the meatballs from heat, garnish them with the sesame seeds and scallions, and serve with the Tare Sauce.

RUBS, MARINADES, SAUCES & STOCKS

Once you learn to master the flame, you'll want to expand your repertoire and introduce new flavors. These recipes help you do just that, providing an easy path to exceptional flavor.

Yield: ½ Cup
Total Time: 5 Minutes

SWEET & SPICY RUB

⅓ cup light brown sugar

1 teaspoon cayenne pepper

1 teaspoon chili powder

1½ teaspoons paprika

2 teaspoons fine sea salt

1 teaspoon garlic powder

1 teaspoon onion powder

1 teaspoon cumin

1 teaspoon black pepper

½ teaspoon mustard powder

¼ teaspoon dried oregano

I. Place all of the ingredients in a bowl, stir to combine, and use immediately or store in an airtight container.

Yield: 4 Cups
Total Time: 5 Minutes

ACAPULCO GOLD RUB

1 cup brown sugar

½ cup kosher salt

½ cup chili powder

¼ cup Hungarian paprika

¼ cup coriander

1 tablespoon ground ginger

¼ cup cumin

⅓ cup garlic powder

⅓ cup onion powder

1 tablespoon lemon zest

¼ cup Dutch cocoa powder

I. Place all of the ingredients in a bowl, stir to combine, and use immediately or store in an airtight container.

Yield: ¼ Cup
Total Time: 5 Minutes

MOLE RUB

1 tablespoon allspice

1½ teaspoons ground cloves

1½ teaspoons cinnamon

1½ teaspoons cumin

1 tablespoon coriander

1 tablespoon ground ginger

I. Place all of the ingredients in a small bowl, stir to combine, and use immediately or store in an airtight container.

Yield: 1½ Cups
Total Time: 5 Minutes

LEMON & HERB POULTRY RUB

1 cup sugar

2 tablespoons kosher salt

2 teaspoons black pepper

2 teaspoons lemon zest

1 tablespoon chopped fresh rosemary

1 tablespoon fresh thyme

1 tablespoon chopped fresh parsley

I. Place all of the ingredients in a bowl, stir to combine, and use immediately or store in an airtight container.

Yield: ½ Cup

Total Time: 5 Minutes

RUSTIC STEAK RUB

6 garlic cloves, minced

2 tablespoons thyme

2 tablespoons kosher salt

1½ tablespoons black pepper

1½ tablespoons white pepper

1 tablespoon red pepper flakes

1 tablespoon sweet paprika

1½ teaspoons onion powder

I. Place all of the ingredients in a bowl, stir to combine, and use immediately or store in an airtight container.

Yield: ¾ Cup

Total Time: 5 Minutes

SMOKED PAPRIKA RUB

¼ cup smoked paprika

4 teaspoons coriander

4 teaspoons cumin

2 teaspoons cayenne pepper

2 tablespoons black pepper

2 tablespoons kosher salt

I. Place all of the ingredients in a bowl, stir to combine, and use immediately or store in an airtight container.

Yield: 1 Cup

Total Time: 5 Minutes

SEAFOOD RUB

1½ tablespoons kosher salt

3 tablespoons paprika

3 tablespoons onion powder

3 tablespoons black pepper

1 tablespoon Cajun seasoning

3 tablespoons turmeric

3 tablespoons coriander

I. Place all of the ingredients in a bowl, stir to combine, and use immediately or store in an airtight container.

Yield: ¾ Cup

Total Time: 5 Minutes

CHILE RUB

½ cup ancho chile powder

1 tablespoon paprika

1 tablespoon black pepper

1 tablespoon kosher salt

2 teaspoons cumin

1 teaspoon cayenne pepper

1 teaspoon mustard powder

1 teaspoon dried oregano

I. Place all of the ingredients in a bowl, stir to combine, and use immediately or store in an airtight container.

Yield: ½ Cup

Total Time: 5 Minutes

FIVE-ALARM RUB

½ habanero chile pepper, stem and seeds removed, minced

1 tablespoon ground star anise

1 tablespoon cinnamon

1 tablespoon ground Sichuan pepper

1 tablespoon ground fennel seeds

1 tablespoon ground cloves

1 tablespoon garlic powder

1 tablespoon ground ginger

1 tablespoon fine sea salt

I. Place all of the ingredients in a bowl, stir to combine, and use immediately or store in an airtight container.

Yield: ¾ Cup

Total Time: 5 Minutes

SMOKY ST. LOUIS RUB

¼ cup paprika

3 tablespoons garlic powder

2 tablespoons black pepper

2 tablespoons kosher salt

2 tablespoons onion powder

1 tablespoon dark brown sugar

1 tablespoon ground ginger

1 tablespoon mustard powder

2 teaspoons liquid smoke

1 teaspoon celery salt

I. Place all of the ingredients in a bowl, stir to combine, and use immediately or store in an airtight container.

Yield: ½ Cup

Total Time: 5 Minutes

KASHMIRI CHILE RUB

3 tablespoons Kashmiri chile powder

3 tablespoons smoked paprika

1 tablespoon dried oregano

2 teaspoons cumin

2 teaspoons black pepper

2 teaspoons fine sea salt

1 teaspoon dried thyme

I. Place all of the ingredients in a bowl, stir to combine, and use immediately or store in an airtight container.

Yield: ½ Cup

Total Time: 5 Minutes

SPICY SOUTHWESTERN RUB

2 tablespoons chili powder

2 tablespoons paprika

1 tablespoon cayenne pepper

1 tablespoon minced habanero pepper

1 tablespoon cumin

1 tablespoon coriander

1 tablespoon grated garlic

1 tablespoon kosher salt

1 tablespoon black pepper

I. Place all of the ingredients in a mixing bowl, stir to combine, and use immediately or store in an airtight container.

KASHMIRI CHILE RUB

See page 201

Yield: 1½ Cups

Total Time: 5 Minutes

BBQ POULTRY RUB

⅓ cup kosher salt

½ cup brown sugar

¼ cup smoked paprika

1 tablespoon cayenne pepper

1 tablespoon chili powder

2 teaspoons cumin

1 tablespoon onion powder

2 tablespoons garlic powder

1 tablespoon black pepper

1 tablespoon ground fennel seeds

1 tablespoon coriander

1 tablespoon dry mustard

I. Place all of the ingredients in a bowl, stir to combine, and use immediately or store in an airtight container.

Yield: ¼ Cup

Total Time: 5 Minutes

BLACKENING SPICE

1½ tablespoons paprika

1 tablespoon chili powder

1 tablespoon cumin

1½ teaspoons coriander

½ teaspoon cayenne pepper

1 tablespoon onion powder

2 teaspoons garlic powder

2 teaspoons black pepper

I. Place all of the ingredients in a mixing bowl, stir to combine, and use immediately or store in an airtight container.

Yield: 1½ Cups
Total Time: 5 Minutes

ZA'ATAR

1 tablespoon cumin

1 tablespoon sumac

1 tablespoon thyme

2 teaspoons hemp seeds

2 teaspoons crushed, toasted sunflower seeds

2 tablespoons sesame seeds

2 tablespoons kosher salt

1 tablespoon black pepper

2 tablespoons chopped fresh oregano

2 tablespoons chopped fresh basil

2 tablespoons chopped fresh parsley

1 tablespoon garlic powder

1 tablespoon onion powder

I. Place all of the ingredients in a bowl, stir to combine, and use immediately or store in an airtight container.

Yield: 1¼ Cups
Total Time: 5 Minutes

BRISKET RUB

½ cup paprika

6 tablespoons black pepper

2 tablespoons chipotle chile powder

2 tablespoons chili powder

4 teaspoons cayenne pepper

2 teaspoons cumin

2 teaspoons dried oregano

1 tablespoon kosher salt

I. Place all of the ingredients in a mixing bowl, stir to combine, and use immediately or store in an airtight container.

BRISKET RUB

See page 205

Yield: 1½ Cups

Total Time: 5 Minutes

JERK MARINADE

1 medium onion, finely diced

¼ cup scallions, trimmed and finely diced

1 scotch bonnet pepper, chopped

3 tablespoons soy sauce

1 tablespoon white vinegar

3 tablespoons extra-virgin olive oil

2 teaspoons fresh thyme

2 teaspoons sugar

1 teaspoon fine sea salt

1 teaspoon black pepper

1 teaspoon allspice

½ teaspoon freshly grated nutmeg

½ teaspoon cinnamon

I. Place all of the ingredients in a food processor, blitz until smooth, and use immediately or store in an airtight container.

Yield: ½ Cup

Total Time: 5 Minutes

CAJUN RUB

¼ cup fine sea salt

2 teaspoons liquid smoke

2 tablespoons black pepper

2 teaspoons smoked paprika

2 teaspoons garlic powder

1 teaspoon onion powder

1 teaspoon cayenne pepper

1 teaspoon dried thyme

I. Place all of the ingredients in a bowl, stir to combine, and use immediately or store in an airtight container.

Yield: 18 Cups
Total Time: 5 Minutes

POULTRY BRINE

16 cups warm water

1 cup fine sea salt

1 cup light brown sugar

¼ cup extra-virgin olive oil

Juice of ½ lemon

4 garlic cloves, crushed

1 tablespoon black pepper

I. Place all of the ingredients in a stockpot and stir to combine. Use immediately or cover until ready to use.

Yield: 2½ Cups
Total Time: 5 Minutes

RED WINE & HERB MARINADE

2 cups red wine

2 tablespoons red wine vinegar

2 garlic cloves, minced

1 tablespoon chopped fresh rosemary

1 teaspoon fresh thyme

½ small white onion, finely diced

1 teaspoon fresh lemon juice

½ teaspoon dried oregano

1 teaspoon black pepper

1 teaspoon fine sea salt

I. Place all of the ingredients in a bowl, whisk to combine, and use immediately or store in an airtight container.

CAJUN RUB

See page 208

Yield: 1½ Cups

Total Time: 5 Minutes

LAMB MARINADE

8 garlic cloves, minced

1 tablespoon cumin

2 tablespoons black pepper

1 tablespoon ground fennel

1 tablespoon paprika

2 tablespoons kosher salt

2 teaspoons Dijon mustard

1 cup extra-virgin olive oil

I.   Place all of the ingredients in a bowl, stir to combine, and use immediately or store in an airtight container.

Yield: 1 Cup

Total Time: 5 Minutes

CITRUS & SAGE MARINADE

3 garlic cloves

⅓ cup fresh sage

Zest and juice of 1 orange

1 tablespoon coriander

1½ teaspoons black pepper

½ teaspoon red pepper flakes

¼ cup extra-virgin olive oil

I.   Place all of the ingredients in a food processor, blitz until combined, and use immediately or store in an airtight container.

Yield: 1½ Cups

Total Time: 5 Minutes

BAY BLEND MARINADE

12 bay leaves

1 onion, chopped

6 garlic cloves, chopped

2 celery stalks, chopped

½ teaspoon allspice

¼ teaspoon cinnamon

½ teaspoon ground ginger

2 teaspoons black pepper

1 tablespoon kosher salt

¼ cup extra-virgin olive oil

I. Place all of the ingredients in a food processor, blitz until smooth, and use immediately or store in the refrigerator.

Yield: 1¾ Cups

Total Time: 5 Minutes

SESAME & HONEY MARINADE

¾ cup kecap manis

½ cup rice vinegar

¼ cup sesame oil

¼ cup honey

1 teaspoon cinnamon

1 teaspoon black pepper

1 teaspoon sesame seeds

I. Place all of the ingredients in a bowl, whisk to combine, and use immediately or store in the refrigerator.

Yield: 1½ Cups

Total Time: 20 Minutes

PERI-PERI MARINADE

1 teaspoon coriander seeds

2 dried chile peppers, stems and seeds removed

1 tablespoon dried oregano

1 tablespoon sweet paprika

Pinch of cinnamon

2 teaspoons Worcestershire sauce

2 garlic cloves, minced

Juice of 1 lime

1 tablespoon honey

2 teaspoons kosher salt

5 tablespoons balsamic vinegar

1 tablespoon water

¼ cup extra-virgin olive oil

1 handful of fresh cilantro, chopped

I. Place the coriander seeds and chiles in a small dry saucepan and toast them over medium heat for 1 minute, shaking the pan occasionally. Stir in the oregano, paprika, cinnamon, Worcestershire sauce, garlic, lime juice, honey, salt, balsamic vinegar, and water and bring the mixture to a simmer. Cook for about 10 minutes.

2. Transfer the mixture to a blender, add the olive oil and cilantro, and blitz until smooth. Let the marinade cool completely before using.

RECADO ROJO

3½ oz. yucateca achiote paste

14 tablespoons fresh lime juice

14 tablespoons orange juice

7 tablespoons grapefruit juice

1 teaspoon dried oregano

1 teaspoon dried marjoram

1 habanero chile pepper, stems and seeds removed

5 garlic cloves

1 cinnamon stick, grated

Salt, to taste

1. Place the achiote paste and juices in a bowl and let the mixture sit for 15 minutes.

2. Place the mixture and the remaining ingredients in a blender and puree until smooth.

3. Taste, adjust the seasoning as needed, and use as desired.

PERI-PERI MARINADE

See page 214

REMOULADE SAUCE

1½ cups mayonnaise

½ cup Creole mustard

Juice of 2 lemons

3 tablespoons sriracha

3 tablespoons sweet relish

¾ teaspoon kosher salt

½ teaspoon black pepper

I. Place all of the ingredients in a bowl and whisk until thoroughly combined. Use immediately or store in the refrigerator.

CHERMOULA SAUCE

1 tablespoon saffron

4 cups mayonnaise

1 tablespoon ras el hanout

1 tablespoon berbere
seasoning

2 tablespoons Za'atar
(see page 205)

1 tablespoon sumac

2 cups chopped fresh herbs
(tarragon, parsley, chives, and
cilantro recommended)

1 tablespoon dried oregano

1 tablespoon kosher salt

1 tablespoon black pepper

1. Place the saffron in ¼ cup water and let it bloom. Remove the saffron from the water and reserve the liquid for another preparation (it's really good in a tomato sauce, for example)—using it in this sauce will make it too loose.

2. Place the saffron and the remaining ingredients in a large bowl and stir until thoroughly combined. Use immediately or transfer to an airtight container and store in the refrigerator.

CHERMOULA SAUCE

See page 219

Yield: 1½ Cups

Total Time: 1 Hour and 30 Minutes

SMOKY SOUTHERN BBQ SAUCE

1 cup hickory woodchips

2 garlic cloves, minced

1 white onion, minced

1 cup crushed tomatoes, drained

¼ cup tomato paste

2 tablespoons white wine vinegar

2 tablespoons balsamic vinegar

1 tablespoon Dijon mustard

Juice from 1 lime

1-inch piece of fresh ginger, peeled and minced

1 teaspoon smoked paprika

½ teaspoon cinnamon

2 dried chipotle peppers, stems and seeds removed, minced

1 habanero pepper, stems and seeds removed, minced

Salt and pepper, to taste

1. Soak the woodchips in a bowl of water for 20 minutes.

2. Prepare a fire, either setting up an even coal bed if you are able to adjust the height of your grate easily, or banking the coals to set up one zone for direct heat and another for indirect. Set up a grate over the coals.

3. Place the garlic, onion, tomatoes, and tomato paste in a food processor and blitz until combined. Add the remaining ingredients and blitz until incorporated. Pour the sauce into a saucepan.

4. Drain the woodchips and spread them over the coals. Place your hand over the grate to test the heat in each section. Place the saucepan over medium heat—a spot you can leave your hand over for 5 seconds before you need to move it away—and bring the sauce to a boil. Let the sauce cook until it has reduced by about one-third, about 20 minutes.

5. Taste, adjust the seasoning if necessary, and use immediately or store in the refrigerator.

Yield: 1½ Cups

Total Time: 30 Minutes

KANSAS CITY BBQ SAUCE

1 tablespoon extra-virgin olive oil

4 garlic cloves, minced

1 cup ketchup

¼ cup water

2 tablespoons molasses

2 tablespoons dark brown sugar

1 tablespoon apple cider vinegar

1 tablespoon Worcestershire sauce

1 bay leaf

1 teaspoon mustard powder

1 teaspoon chili powder

1 teaspoon onion powder

1 teaspoon liquid smoke

1 teaspoon black pepper

1 teaspoon kosher salt

1. Place the olive oil in a saucepan and warm it over medium-high heat. Add the garlic and cook, stirring continually, for 1 minute.

2. Stir in the remaining ingredients and bring the sauce to a boil. Reduce the heat to medium and simmer until the sauce has reduced by one-third, about 20 minutes.

3. Remove the bay leaf and discard it. Taste, adjust the seasoning if necessary, and use immediately, or let the sauce cool and store it in the refrigerator.

Yield: 2 Cups

Total Time: 30 Minutes

SOUTH CAROLINA BBQ SAUCE

1 cup yellow mustard

½ cup honey

½ cup apple cider vinegar

2 tablespoons ketchup

1 tablespoon light brown sugar

2 teaspoons Worcestershire sauce

3 garlic cloves, minced

1 teaspoon ground black pepper

Salt, to taste

1. Place all of the ingredients in a saucepan, stir to combine, and bring to a boil over medium-high heat. Reduce the heat to medium and cook until the sauce has reduced by one-third, about 20 minutes.

2. Taste, adjust the seasoning if necessary, and use immediately, or let the sauce cool and store it in the refrigerator.

Yield: 2 Cups

Total Time: 30 Minutes

COFFEE & BOURBON BBQ SAUCE

2 cups brewed coffee

¼ cup dark brown sugar

¾ cup bourbon

3 tablespoons molasses

¼ cup apple cider vinegar

2 tablespoons Worcestershire sauce

¼ cup ketchup

1 tablespoon granulated garlic

½ tablespoon black pepper

1 tablespoon cornstarch

1. Place all of the ingredients in a saucepan, stir to combine, and bring the sauce to a boil over medium-high heat. Reduce the heat to medium and simmer the sauce until it has reduced by one-third, about 20 minutes.

2. Taste, adjust the seasoning as necessary, and use immediately, or let the sauce cool and store it in the refrigerator.

Yield: 1½ Cups

Total Time: 30 Minutes

MOLASSES BBQ SAUCE

½ cup ketchup

¼ cup dark brown sugar

2 tablespoons granulated sugar

2 tablespoons Dijon mustard

3 tablespoons apple cider vinegar

2 garlic cloves, minced

¼ cup blackstrap molasses

¼ teaspoon ground cloves

½ teaspoon hot sauce

¼ cup honey

I. Place all of the ingredients in a medium saucepan and bring to a boil over medium-high heat. Reduce the heat so that the sauce simmers and cook, stirring occasionally, until the sauce has reduced by one-third, about 20 minutes.

2. Taste, adjust the seasoning as necessary, and use immediately, or let the sauce cool and store it in the refrigerator.

Yield: 2 Cups

Total Time: 30 Minutes

TARE SAUCE

½ cup Chicken Stock
(see page 245)

½ cup soy sauce

½ cup mirin

¼ cup sake

½ cup brown sugar

2 smashed garlic cloves

1 tablespoon minced ginger

2 scallions, trimmed
and sliced

I. Place all of the ingredients in a small saucepan and bring to a simmer over low heat. Simmer for 10 minutes, stirring once or twice.

2. Remove the pan from heat and let the sauce cool completely. Strain before using or storing.

SALSA VERDE

1 lb. tomatillos, husked and rinsed

5 garlic cloves, unpeeled

1 small white onion, quartered

10 serrano chile peppers

2 bunches of fresh cilantro

Salt, to taste

1. Warm a cast-iron skillet over high heat. Place the tomatillos, garlic, onion, and chiles in the pan and cook until charred all over, turning them occasionally.

2. Remove the vegetables from the pan and let them cool slightly.

3. Peel the garlic cloves and remove the stems and seeds from the chiles. Place the charred vegetables in a blender, add the cilantro, and puree until smooth.

4. Season the salsa with salt and enjoy.

Yield: 1 Cup
Total Time: 25 Minutes

PICO DE GALLO

2 large tomatoes, finely diced

½ onion, finely diced

2 jalapeño chile peppers, stems and seeds removed, finely diced

Salt, to taste

1 cup fresh cilantro, chopped

I. Place the tomatoes, onion, and chiles in a small mixing bowl and stir to combine. Season the pico de gallo with salt, stir in the cilantro, and refrigerate the salsa for 15 minutes before serving.

Yield: 1 Cup

Total Time: 5 Minutes

ROMESCO SAUCE

2 large roasted red bell peppers

1 garlic clove, smashed

½ cup slivered almonds, toasted

¼ cup tomato puree

2 tablespoons finely chopped flat-leaf parsley

2 tablespoons sherry vinegar

1 teaspoon smoked paprika

Salt and pepper, to taste

½ cup extra-virgin olive oil

1. Place all of the ingredients, except for the olive oil, in a blender or food processor and pulse until the mixture is smooth.

2. Add the olive oil in a steady stream and blitz until emulsified. Season with salt and pepper and use immediately.

CHIMICHURRI SAUCE

1 cup fresh parsley

2 large garlic cloves, smashed

1 teaspoon dried thyme

¼ teaspoon red pepper flakes

½ cup water

¼ cup white wine vinegar

¼ cup extra-virgin olive oil

1 teaspoon fine sea salt

⅛ teaspoon black pepper

I. Use a mortar and pestle or a food processor to combine the ingredients until the sauce has the desired texture. Use immediately or store in the refrigerator.

CHIMICHURRI SAUCE

See page 237

Yield: ¾ Cup

Total Time: 10 Minutes

CLARIFIED BUTTER

1 cup unsalted butter

I. Place the butter in a saucepan and melt it over medium heat.

2. Reduce the heat to the lowest possible setting. Cook until the butter fat is very clear, and the milk solids drop to the bottom of the pan.

3. Skim the foam from the surface of the butter and discard it. Transfer the butter to a container and refrigerate until ready to use.

Yield: ½ Cup
Total Time: 25 Minutes

BALSAMIC GLAZE

1 cup balsamic vinegar

¼ cup brown sugar

1. Place the vinegar and sugar in a small saucepan and bring the mixture to a boil.

2. Reduce the heat to medium-low and simmer for 8 to 10 minutes, stirring frequently, until the mixture has thickened.

3. Remove the pan from heat and let the glaze cool for 15 minutes before using.

Yield: 8 Cups

Total Time: 6 Hours

CHICKEN STOCK

7 lbs. chicken bones, rinsed

4 cups chopped yellow onions

2 cups chopped carrots

2 cups chopped celery

3 garlic cloves, crushed

3 sprigs of fresh thyme

1 teaspoon black peppercorns

1 bay leaf

I. Place the chicken bones in a stockpot and cover them with cold water. Bring to a simmer over medium-high heat and use a ladle to skim off any impurities that rise to the surface.

2. Add the vegetables, thyme, peppercorns, and bay leaf, reduce the heat to low, and simmer for 5 hours, skimming the stock occasionally to remove any impurities that rise to the surface.

3. Strain the stock, let it cool slightly, and transfer it to the refrigerator. Leave the stock uncovered and let it cool completely. Remove the layer of fat and cover. The stock will keep in the refrigerator for 3 to 5 days, and in the freezer for up to 3 months.

Yield: 6 Cups

Total Time: 4 Hours

FISH STOCK

¼ cup extra-virgin olive oil

1 leek, trimmed, rinsed well, and chopped

1 large yellow onion, unpeeled, root cleaned, chopped

2 large carrots, chopped

1 celery stalk, chopped

¾ lb. whitefish bodies

4 sprigs of fresh parsley

3 sprigs of fresh thyme

2 bay leaves

1 teaspoon black peppercorns

1 teaspoon kosher salt

8 cups water

1. Place the olive oil in a stockpot and warm it over low heat. Add the vegetables and cook until the liquid they release has evaporated.

2. Add the whitefish bodies, the aromatics, the salt, and the water to the pot, raise the heat to high, and bring to a boil. Reduce the heat so that the stock simmers and cook for 3 hours, skimming to remove any impurities that float to the surface.

3. Strain the stock through a fine sieve, let it cool slightly, and place it in the refrigerator, uncovered, to chill. When the stock is completely cool, remove the fat layer from the top and cover. The stock will keep in the refrigerator for 3 to 5 days, and in the freezer for up to 3 months.

BEEF STOCK

7 lbs. beef bones, rinsed

4 cups chopped yellow onions

2 cups chopped carrots

2 cups chopped celery

3 garlic cloves, crushed

3 sprigs of fresh thyme

1 teaspoon black peppercorns

1 bay leaf

1. Place the beef bones in a stockpot and cover them with cold water. Bring to a simmer over medium-high heat and use a ladle to skim off any impurities that rise to the surface.

2. Add the vegetables, thyme, peppercorns, and bay leaf, reduce the heat to low, and simmer for 5 hours, occasionally skimming the stock to remove any impurities that rise to the surface.

3. Strain the stock, let it cool slightly, and transfer it to the refrigerator. Leave the stock uncovered and let it cool completely. Remove the layer of fat and cover. The stock will keep in the refrigerator for 3 to 5 days, and in the freezer for up to 3 months.

METRIC CONVERSIONS

US MEASUREMENT	APPROXIMATE METRIC LIQUID MEASUREMENT	APPROXIMATE METRIC DRY MEASUREMENT
1 teaspoon	5 ml	5 g
1 tablespoon or ½ ounce	15 ml	14 g
1 ounce or ⅛ cup	30 ml	29 g
¼ cup or 2 ounces	60 ml	57 g
⅓ cup	80 ml	76 g
½ cup or 4 ounces	120 ml	113 g
⅔ cup	160 ml	151 g
¾ cup or 6 ounces	180 ml	170 g
1 cup or 8 ounces or ½ pint	240 ml	227 g
1½ cups or 12 ounces	350 ml	340 g
2 cups or 1 pint or 16 ounces	475 ml	454 g
3 cups or 1½ pints	700 ml	680 g
4 cups or 2 pints or 1 quart	950 ml	908 g

INDEX

A

Acapulco Gold Rub, 196
almonds
    Romesco de Peix, 112
    Romesco Sauce, 236
American cheese
    Bacon Cheeseburgers, 43
andouille sausage
    Jambalaya, 116
    Shrimp Boil, 119
appetizers & sides
    Buffalo Wings, 187
    Cantaloupe & Mozzarella with Balsamic
      Glaze, 144
    Charred Eggplant, 161
    Chicken Tsukune, 192
    Chorizo-Stuffed Mushrooms, 175
    Corn Tortillas, 180
    Elotes, 152
    Fire-Roasted Peppers & Onions, 164
    Grilled Beets with Dukkah, 149
    Grilled Cabbage, 159
    Grilled Goat Cheese, 176
    Grilled Leeks with Romesco, 168
    Grilled Oysters, 155
    Grilled Romaine & Sweet Potato, 169
    Grilled Sardines with Lemon & Herbs,
      177
    Musaengchae, 154
    Pita Bread, 191
    Raita, 148
    Smoky & Spicy Chicken Wings, 186
    Spicy Turkey Wings, 172
    Succotash, 183
    Vegetable Kebabs, 147
apples
    Grilled Romaine & Sweet Potato, 169
    Pork & Apple Casserole, 97
apricots, dried
    Chicken Tagine, 70
Asparagus, Grilled, 167

B

bacon/bacon fat
    Bacon Cheeseburgers, 43
    BBQ Burgers, 44
    Brown Sugar Ribs, 78
    Manhattan Clam Chowder, 136
    Succotash, 183
Balsamic Glaze
    Cantaloupe & Mozzarella with Balsamic
      Glaze, 144
    recipe, 242
basil
    Succotash, 183
    Whole Branzino, 107
Bay Blend Marinade, 213
BBQ Brisket, 39
BBQ Burgers, 44
BBQ Poultry Rub, 204
BBQ Sauce
    BBQ Burgers, 44
    Brown Sugar Ribs, 78
BBQ Shrimp, New Orleans Style, 128
beef
    Bacon Cheeseburgers, 43
    BBQ Brisket, 39
    BBQ Burgers, 44
    Beef Kebabs, 47
    Beef Shawarma, 51
    Beef Stock, 249
    Braised Short Ribs, 50
    Carne Asada, 48
    Chile-Rubbed London Broil, 28
    Chipotle T-Bone, 22
    Coffee-Rubbed Sirloin, 31
    Filet Mignon, 32
    Flank Steak, 27
    New York Strip, 19
    Porterhouse, 23
    Prime Rib, 40
    Red Wine & Herb Tri-Tip Steak, 36
    Rib Eye, 20
    Strip Steaks with Peppercorn Cream
      Sauce, 35

Beef Stock
    Braised Short Ribs, 50
    recipe, 249
Beets with Dukkah, Grilled, 149
berbere seasoning
    Chermoula Sauce, 219
Blackened Salmon, 106
Blackening Spice
    Blackened Salmon, 106
    recipe, 204
Bourbon BBQ Sauce, Coffee &, 228
Braised Short Ribs, 50
Branzino, Whole, 107
Brisket Rub
    BBQ Brisket, 39
    recipe, 205
Brown Sugar Ribs, 78
brushes, 15
buckets, 15
Buffalo Wings, 187
burgers
    Bacon Cheeseburgers, 43
    BBQ Burgers, 44
    Chicken Teriyaki Burgers, 80

C

cabbage
    Coleslaw, 184
    Grilled Cabbage, 159
Cajun Rub
    Cajun Tilapia, 120
    recipe, 208
Cantaloupe & Mozzarella with Balsamic
    Glaze, 144
Carne Asada, 48
Carnitas, 102
carrots
    Beef Stock, 249
    Braised Short Ribs, 50
    Chicken Stock, 245
    Chicken Tagine, 70
    Coleslaw, 184
    Fish Stock, 246
    Potjiekos, 65

Split Pea Soup with Smoked Ham, 94
Cedar-Plank Salmon, 129
celery
    Bay Blend Marinade, 213
    Beef Stock, 249
    Buffalo Wings, 187
    Chicken Stock, 245
    Fish Stock, 246
    Jambalaya, 116
    Manhattan Clam Chowder, 136
    Salmon & Vegetable Skewers, 132
    Split Pea Soup with Smoked Ham, 94
charcoal, 10, 13
charcoal chimneys, 14
Charred Eggplant, 161
cheddar cheese
    BBQ Burgers, 44
cheese. see individual cheese types
Chermoula Sauce
    Chermoula Sea Bass, 138
    recipe, 219
chicken
    Buffalo Wings, 187
    Chicken Kebab, 73
    Chicken Souvlaki, 81
    Chicken Tagine, 70
    Chicken Teriyaki Burgers, 80
    Chicken Tsukune, 192
    Jamaican Jerk Chicken, 72
    Jambalaya, 116
    Peri-Peri Chicken, 69
    Peri-Peri Marinade, 214
    Rotisserie Chicken, 86
    Smoky & Spicy Chicken Wings, 186
    Spatchcock Za'atar Chicken, 89
Chicken Stock
    Chicken Tagine, 70
    Chorizo-Stuffed Mushrooms, 175
    Jambalaya, 116
    Lamb Sharba, 53
    Octopus al Pastor, 126–127
    recipe, 245
    Split Pea Soup with Smoked Ham, 94
    Tare Sauce, 231
chickpeas
    Lamb Sharba, 53
Chile Rub
    Chile-Rubbed London Broil, 28
    recipe, 199
Chimichurri Sauce
    Grilled Lamb Loin with Chimichurri, 57
    recipe, 237
Chipotle T-Bone, 22
chorizo. see sausage
Chorizo-Stuffed Mushrooms, 175
cilantro
    Carne Asada, 48
    Carnitas, 102
    Elotes, 152
    Grilled Oysters, 155
    Grilled Sardines with Lemon & Herbs,
        177

Lobster Mojo de Ajo, 124
Peri-Peri Marinade, 214
Pico de Gallo, 234
Raita, 148
Romesco de Peix, 112
Salsa Verde, 233
Citrus & Sage Marinade, 212
clams
    Lobster Cioppino, 114–115
    Manhattan Clam Chowder, 136
Clarified Butter
    Buffalo Wings, 187
    recipe, 241
cocoa powder
    Acapulco Gold Rub, 196
coffee
    Coffee & Bourbon BBQ Sauce, 228
    Coffee-Rubbed Sirloin, 31
Cognac
    Strip Steaks with Peppercorn Cream
        Sauce, 35
Coleslaw
    BBQ Brisket, 39
    recipe, 184
corn
    Elotes, 152
    Succotash, 183
Corn Tortillas
    Carnitas, 102
    Octopus al Pastor, 126–127
    recipe, 180
couscous
    Chicken Tagine, 70
cucumber
    Beef Shawarma, 51
    Raita, 148

D
daikon radish
    Musaengchae, 154
direct heat, 12
doneness, determining, 9
Dukkah, Grilled Beets with, 149
Dwaeji Bulgogi, 90

E
Eggplant, Charred, 161
Elotes, 152
epazote
    Octopus al Pastor, 126–127

F
fennel
    Lobster Cioppino, 114–115
    Tuna with Orange & Fennel Salad, 133
feta cheese
    Grilled Romaine & Sweet Potato, 169
    Summer Squash Salad, 160
Fig & Goat Cheese Salad, 145
Filet Mignon, 32
fire

building and tending, 10–12
Fire-Roasted Peppers & Onions, 164
fish and seafood
    BBQ Shrimp, New Orleans Style, 128
    Blackened Salmon, 106
    Cajun Tilapia, 120
    Cedar-Plank Salmon, 129
    Chermoula Sea Bass, 138
    Fish Stock, 246
    Grilled Oysters, 155
    Grilled Sardines with Lemon & Herbs,
        177
    Honey & Soy–Glazed Rainbow Trout,
        121
    Jambalaya, 116
    Lobster Cioppino, 114–115
    Lobster Mojo de Ajo, 124
    Manhattan Clam Chowder, 136
    Mussels in White Wine & Herbs, 111
    Octopus al Pastor, 126–127
    Romesco de Peix, 112
    Salmon & Vegetable Skewers, 132
    Shrimp Boil, 119
    Swordfish, 139
    Tuna with Orange & Fennel Salad, 133
    Whole Branzino, 107
Fish Stock
    Lobster Cioppino, 114–115
    recipe, 246
    Romesco de Peix, 112
Five-Alarm Rub, 200
Flank Steak, 27

G
garlic
    Bay Blend Marinade, 213
    Beef Stock, 249
    Buffalo Wings, 187
    Carne Asada, 48
    Chicken Souvlaki, 81
    Chicken Stock, 245
    Chicken Tagine, 70
    Chimichurri Sauce, 237
    Citrus & Sage Marinade, 212
    Dwaeji Bulgogi, 90
    Grilled Sardines with Lemon & Herbs,
        177
    Jambalaya, 116
    Kansas City BBQ Sauce, 224
    Lamb Kebabs, 62
    Lamb Marinade, 212
    Lobster Cioppino, 114–115
    Lobster Mojo de Ajo, 124
    Manhattan Clam Chowder, 136
    Molasses BBQ Sauce, 230
    Mussels in White Wine & Herbs, 111
    Octopus al Pastor, 126–127
    Peri-Peri Marinade, 214
    Potjiekos, 65
    Poultry Brine, 209
    Prime Rib, 40
    Recado Rojo, 215

Red Wine & Herb Marinade, 209
Rogan Josh, 61
Rosemary & Lemon Leg of Lamb, 56
Rustic Steak Rub, 198
Salmon & Vegetable Skewers, 132
Salsa Verde, 233
Shrimp Boil, 119
Smoky & Spicy Chicken Wings, 186
Smoky Southern BBQ Sauce, 223
South Carolina BBQ Sauce, 227
Tare Sauce, 231
Vegetable Kebabs, 147
ginger, fresh
    Chicken Tagine, 70
    Dwaeji Bulgogi, 90
    Rogan Josh, 61
    Smoky Southern BBQ Sauce, 223
    Tare Sauce, 231
goat cheese
    Elotes, 152
    Fig & Goat Cheese Salad, 145
    Grilled Goat Cheese, 176
gochugaru
    Musaengchae, 154
gochujang
    Dwaeji Bulgogi, 90
grapefruit juice
    Recado Rojo, 215
grates
    cleaning, 9
    raising and lowering, 12, 14
grill brushes, 15
Grilled Asparagus, 167
Grilled Beets with Dukkah, 149
Grilled Cabbage, 159
Grilled Goat Cheese, 176
Grilled Lamb Loin with Chimichurri, 57
Grilled Leeks with Romesco, 168
Grilled Oysters, 155
Grilled Pineapple
    Jamaican Jerk Chicken, 72
Grilled Romaine & Sweet Potato, 169
Grilled Sardines with Lemon & Herbs, 177

H

halibut
    Lobster Cioppino, 114–115
Ham, Split Pea Soup with Smoked, 94
hatchets, 15
hazelnuts
    Grilled Beets with Dukkah, 149
honey
    Cedar-Plank Salmon, 129
    Coleslaw, 184
    Honey & Soy–Glazed Rainbow Trout,
      121
    Molasses BBQ Sauce, 230
    Sesame & Honey Marinade, 213
    South Carolina BBQ Sauce, 227
    Vegetable Kebabs, 147
hot sauce
    Buffalo Wings, 187

Spicy Turkey Wings, 172

I

indirect heat, 13

J

jalapeños
    BBQ Burgers, 44
    Carne Asada, 48
    see also peppers, chile
Jamaican Jerk Chicken, 72
Jambalaya, 116
Jerk Marinade
    Jamaican Jerk Chicken, 72
    recipe, 208

K

Kansas City BBQ Sauce, 224
Kashmiri Chile Rub
    recipe, 201
    Spicy Lamb Chops with Raita, 54
kecap manis
    Sesame & Honey Marinade, 213
kiln-dried wood, 10

L

lamb
    Grilled Lamb Loin with Chimichurri, 57
    Lamb Kebabs, 62
    Lamb Sharba, 53
    Potjiekos, 65
    Rogan Josh, 61
    Rosemary & Lemon Leg of Lamb, 56
    Spicy Lamb Chops with Raita, 54
Lamb Marinade
    Grilled Lamb Loin with Chimichurri, 57
    recipe, 212
leeks
    Fish Stock, 246
    Grilled Leeks with Romesco, 168
lemons/lemon juice
    Beef Shawarma, 51
    Grilled Sardines with Lemon & Herbs,
      177
    Lemon & Herb Poultry Rub, 197
    Remoulade Sauce, 218
    Rosemary & Lemon Leg of Lamb, 56
lettuce
    Dwaeji Bulgogi, 90
    Grilled Romaine & Sweet Potato, 169
lima beans
    Succotash, 183
lime juice
    Recado Rojo, 215
    Smoky Southern BBQ Sauce, 223
lobster
    Lobster Cioppino, 114–115
    Lobster Mojo de Ajo, 124

M

Maillard reaction, 8
Manhattan Clam Chowder, 136
maple syrup
    Cedar-Plank Salmon, 129
marinades
    Bay Blend Marinade, 213
    Citrus & Sage Marinade, 212
    Jerk Marinade, 208
    Lamb Marinade, 212
    Peri-Peri Marinade, 214
    Red Wine & Herb Marinade, 209
    Sesame & Honey Marinade, 213
masa harina
    Corn Tortillas, 180
mesclun greens
    Tuna with Orange & Fennel Salad, 133
metric conversions, 250
mint
    Beef Shawarma, 51
    Lamb Sharba, 53
mirin
    Chicken Tsukune, 192
    Tare Sauce, 231
molasses
    Coffee & Bourbon BBQ Sauce, 228
    Kansas City BBQ Sauce, 224
    Molasses BBQ Sauce, 230
    Slow-Cooked Molasses BBQ Ribs, 77
Molasses BBQ Sauce
    recipe, 230
    Slow-Cooked Molasses BBQ Ribs, 77
Mole Rub, 197
monkfish
    Romesco de Peix, 112
Mozzarella with Balsamic Glaze,
  Cantaloupe &, 144
Musaengchae
    Dwaeji Bulgogi, 90
    recipe, 154
mushrooms
    Chorizo-Stuffed Mushrooms, 175
    South Carolina BBQ Sauce, 227
    Vegetable Kebabs, 147
mussels
    Lobster Cioppino, 114–115
    Mussels in White Wine & Herbs, 111
    Romesco de Peix, 112
mustard
    Cedar-Plank Salmon, 129
    Remoulade Sauce, 218

N

New York Strip, 19
nuts. see individual nut types

O

Octopus al Pastor, 126–127
olives
    Grilled Goat Cheese, 176

onions
Bay Blend Marinade, 213
Beef Kebabs, 47
Beef Shawarma, 51
Beef Stock, 249
Braised Short Ribs, 50
Charred Eggplant, 161
Chicken Stock, 245
Chicken Tagine, 70
Chorizo-Stuffed Mushrooms, 175
Fire-Roasted Peppers & Onions, 164
Fish Stock, 246
Jambalaya, 116
Jerk Marinade, 208
Lamb Kebabs, 62
Lamb Sharba, 53
Manhattan Clam Chowder, 136
Octopus al Pastor, 126–127
Pico de Gallo, 234
Potjiekos, 65
Red Wine & Herb Marinade, 209
Rogan Josh, 61
Romesco de Peix, 112
Salsa Verde, 233
Smoky Southern BBQ Sauce, 223
Split Pea Soup with Smoked Ham, 94
Succotash, 183
Tuna with Orange & Fennel Salad, 133
oranges/orange juice
Carne Asada, 48
Citrus & Sage Marinade, 212
Fig & Goat Cheese Salad, 145
Octopus al Pastor, 126–127
Potjiekos, 65
Recado Rojo, 215
Spicy Orange Pork, 91
Tuna with Orange & Fennel Salad, 133
orzo
Lamb Sharba, 53
Oysters, Grilled, 155

P

Parmesan cheese
Chorizo-Stuffed Mushrooms, 175
parsley
BBQ Shrimp, New Orleans Style, 128
Chimichurri Sauce, 237
Chorizo-Stuffed Mushrooms, 175
Grilled Sardines with Lemon & Herbs, 177
Mussels in White Wine & Herbs, 111
Salmon & Vegetable Skewers, 132
Shrimp Boil, 119
Smoky & Spicy Chicken Wings, 186
Split Pea Soup with Smoked Ham, 94
Strip Steaks with Peppercorn Cream Sauce, 35
Tuna with Orange & Fennel Salad, 133
Pea Soup with Smoked Ham, Split, 94
Peppercorn Cream Sauce, Strip Steaks with, 35
peppers, bell

Charred Eggplant, 161
Fire-Roasted Peppers & Onions, 164
Jambalaya, 116
Manhattan Clam Chowder, 136
Romesco de Peix, 112
Romesco Sauce, 236
Salmon & Vegetable Skewers, 132
Vegetable Kebabs, 147
peppers, chile
BBQ Burgers, 44
Carne Asada, 48
Elotes, 152
Five-Alarm Rub, 200
Jerk Marinade, 208
Octopus al Pastor, 126–127
Peri-Peri Marinade, 214
Pico de Gallo, 234
Recado Rojo, 215
Salsa Verde, 233
Smoky Southern BBQ Sauce, 223
Spicy Southwestern Rub, 201
Peri-Peri Marinade
Peri-Peri Chicken, 69
recipe, 214
Pico de Gallo, 234
pineapple/pineapple juice
Chicken Teriyaki Burgers, 80
Octopus al Pastor, 126–127
pistachios
Grilled Beets with Dukkah, 149
Pita Bread
Beef Shawarma, 51
Chicken Souvlaki, 81
Lamb Kebabs, 62
recipe, 191
PK Grill, 14
Porchetta, 98
pork
Brown Sugar Ribs, 78
Carnitas, 102
Dwaeji Bulgogi, 90
Porchetta, 98
Pork & Apple Casserole, 97
Pork Chops, 99
Slow-Cooked Molasses BBQ Ribs, 77
Spicy Orange Pork, 91
Porterhouse, 23
potatoes
Potjiekos, 65
Shrimp Boil, 119
Potjiekos, 65
Poultry Brine
recipe, 209
Rotisserie Chicken, 86
Prime Rib, 40

R

Raita
recipe, 148
Spicy Lamb Chops with Raita, 54
Recado Rojo
Octopus al Pastor, 126–127

recipe, 215
Red Wine & Herb Marinade
recipe, 209
Red Wine & Herb Tri-Tip Steak, 36
Remoulade Sauce
recipe, 218
Shrimp Boil, 119
Rib Eye, 20
ribs
Braised Short Ribs, 50
Brown Sugar Ribs, 78
Slow-Cooked Molasses BBQ Ribs, 77
rice
Dwaeji Bulgogi, 90
Jambalaya, 116
Rogan Josh, 61
Romesco de Peix, 112
Romesco Sauce
Grilled Leeks with Romesco, 168
recipe, 236
rosemary
Beef Kebabs, 47
Braised Short Ribs, 50
Flank Steak, 27
Porchetta, 98
Pork & Apple Casserole, 97
Prime Rib, 40
Rosemary & Lemon Leg of Lamb, 56
Rotisserie Chicken, 86
rotisseries, 14
rubs
Acapulco Gold Rub, 196
BBQ Poultry Rub, 204
Blackening Spice, 204
Brisket Rub, 205
Cajun Rub, 208
Chile Rub, 199
Five-Alarm Rub, 200
Kashmiri Chile Rub, 201
Lemon & Herb Poultry Rub, 197
Mole Rub, 197
Rustic Steak Rub, 198
Seafood Rub, 199
Smoked Paprika Rub, 198
Smoky St. Louis Rub, 200
Spicy Southwestern Rub, 201
Sweet & Spicy Rub, 196
Za'atar, 205
Rustic Steak Rub, 198

S

saffron
Chermoula Sauce, 219
sage
Citrus & Sage Marinade, 212
Porchetta, 98
sake
Chicken Tsukune, 192
Tare Sauce, 231
salads
Fig & Goat Cheese Salad, 145
Summer Squash Salad, 160

Tuna with Orange & Fennel Salad, 133
salmon
    Blackened Salmon, 106
    Cedar-Plank Salmon, 129
    Salmon & Vegetable Skewers, 132
Salsa Verde, 233
Santa Maria grills, 14
sauces
    Balsamic Glaze, 242
    Chermoula Sauce, 219
    Chimichurri Sauce, 237
    Coffee & Bourbon BBQ Sauce, 228
    Kansas City BBQ Sauce, 224
    Molasses BBQ Sauce, 230
    Pico de Gallo, 234
    Remoulade Sauce, 218
    Romesco Sauce, 236
    Salsa Verde, 233
    Smoky Southern BBQ Sauce, 223
    South Carolina BBQ Sauce, 227
    Tare Sauce, 231
sausage
    Chorizo-Stuffed Mushrooms, 175
    Jambalaya, 116
    Shrimp Boil, 119
scallions
    Chicken Tsukune, 192
    Dwaeji Bulgogi, 90
    Jambalaya, 116
    Jerk Marinade, 208
    Tare Sauce, 231
Sea Bass, Chermoula, 138
seafood. see fish and seafood
Seafood Rub
    recipe, 199
    Swordfish, 139
sear, 8
Sesame & Honey Marinade, 213
shallots
    Grilled Sardines with Lemon & Herbs, 177
    Lobster Cioppino, 114–115
    Mussels in White Wine & Herbs, 111
    Prime Rib, 40
    Strip Steaks with Peppercorn Cream Sauce, 35
sherry
    Romesco de Peix, 112
shovels, 15
shrimp
    BBQ Shrimp, New Orleans Style, 128
    Jambalaya, 116
    Shrimp Boil, 119
sides. see appetizers & sides
Slow-Cooked Molasses BBQ Ribs, 77
smoke
    color of, 9
    importance of, 8
Smoked Paprika Rub, 198
Smoky & Spicy Chicken Wings, 186
Smoky Southern BBQ Sauce, 223
Smoky St. Louis Rub, 200

soups and stews
    Lobster Cioppino, 114–115
    Manhattan Clam Chowder, 136
    Romesco de Peix, 112
    Split Pea Soup with Smoked Ham, 94
South Carolina BBQ Sauce, 227
soy sauce
    Dwaeji Bulgogi, 90
    Honey & Soy–Glazed Rainbow Trout, 121
    Tare Sauce, 231
    Tuna with Orange & Fennel Salad, 133
Spatchcock Turkey, 85
Spatchcock Za'atar Chicken, 89
Spicy Lamb Chops with Raita, 54
Spicy Orange Pork, 91
Spicy Southwestern Rub, 201
Spicy Turkey Wings, 172
spinach
    Potjiekos, 65
    Summer Squash Salad, 160
Split Pea Soup with Smoked Ham, 94
Squash Salad, Summer, 160
sriracha
    Remoulade Sauce, 218
Strip Steaks with Peppercorn Cream Sauce, 35
Succotash, 183
sumac
    Chermoula Sauce, 219
Summer Squash Salad, 160
Sweet & Spicy Rub, 196
sweet potatoes
    Grilled Romaine & Sweet Potato, 169
    Potjiekos, 65
Swordfish, 139

T

Tare Sauce
    Chicken Tsukune, 192
    recipe, 231
temperature control, 12–13
Teriyaki Burgers, Chicken, 80
thyme
    Braised Short Ribs, 50
    Flank Steak, 27
    Porchetta, 98
    Pork & Apple Casserole, 97
    Prime Rib, 40
Tilapia, Cajun, 120
tomatoes
    Beef Shawarma, 51
    Chorizo-Stuffed Mushrooms, 175
    Jambalaya, 116
    Lamb Sharba, 53
    Lobster Cioppino, 114–115
    Manhattan Clam Chowder, 136
    Pico de Gallo, 234
    Rogan Josh, 61
    Romesco de Peix, 112
    Romesco Sauce, 236
    Salmon & Vegetable Skewers, 132

Smoky Southern BBQ Sauce, 223
Succotash, 183
Summer Squash Salad, 160
tongs, 15
tools, 14–15
Trout, Honey & Soy–Glazed Rainbow, 121
Tuna with Orange & Fennel Salad, 133
turkey
    Spatchcock Turkey, 85
    Spicy Turkey Wings, 172

V

Vegetable Kebabs, 147

W

walnuts
    Grilled Beets with Dukkah, 149
    Grilled Goat Cheese, 176
Webers, 14
Whole Branzino, 107
wine, red
    Braised Short Ribs, 50
    Fig & Goat Cheese Salad, 145
    Lobster Cioppino, 114–115
    Red Wine & Herb Marinade, 209
    Red Wine & Herb Tri-Tip Steak, 36
wine, white
    Chicken Souvlaki, 81
    Chicken Tagine, 70
    Lobster Cioppino, 114–115
    Mussels in White Wine & Herbs, 111
wood, 10, 12

Y

yams
    Potjiekos, 65
yogurt
    Beef Shawarma, 51
    Chicken Kebab, 73
    Grilled Beets with Dukkah, 149
    Lamb Kebabs, 62
    Raita, 148
    Rogan Josh, 61
yucateca achiote paste
    Recado Rojo, 215

Z

Za'atar
    Chermoula Sauce, 219
    recipe, 205
    Spatchcock Za'atar Chicken, 89
zucchini
    Summer Squash Salad, 160
    Vegetable Kebabs, 147

ABOUT CIDER MILL PRESS BOOK PUBLISHERS

Good ideas ripen with time. From seed to harvest, Cider Mill Press brings fine reading, information, and entertainment together between the covers of its creatively crafted books. Our Cider Mill bears fruit twice a year, publishing a new crop of titles each spring and fall.

"Where Good Books Are Ready for Press"

501 Nelson Place
Nashville, Tennessee 37214

cidermillpress.com